Women and the Limits of Citizenship in the French Revolution

The French masses overwhelmingly supported the Revolution in 1789. Economic hardship, hunger, and debt combined to put them solidly behind the leaders. But between the people's expectations and the politicians' interpretation of what was needed to construct a new state lay a vast chasm. Olwen H. Hufton explores the reponses of two groups of working women – those in rural areas and those in Paris – to the revolution's aftermath.

Women were denied citizenship in the new state, but they were not apolitical. In Paris, collective female activity promoted a controlled economy as women struggled to secure an adequate supply of bread at a reasonable price. Rural women engaged in collective confrontation to undermine government religious policy which was destroying the networks of traditional Catholic charity.

Hufton examines the motivations of these two groups, the strategies they used to advance their respective causes, and the bitter misogynistic legacy of the republican tradition which persisted into the twentieth century.

OLWEN H. HUFTON is professor of European History and Women's Studies at Harvard University.

D0003708

Women and the Limits of Citizenship in the French Revolution

The
Donald G. Creighton Lectures
1989

OLWEN H. HUFTON

UNIVERSITY OF TORONTO PRESS
Toronto Buffalo London

© Olwen H. Hufton 1992
Printed in Canada

ISBN 0-8020-5898-1 (cloth)
ISBN 0-8020-6837-5 (paper)

Paperback reprinted 1994, 1999

Printed on acid-free paper

Canadian Cataloguing in Publication Data

Hufton, Olwen H.
Women and the limits of citizenship in the
French Revolution

(The Donald G. Creighton lectures)
Includes bibliographical references.
ISBN 0-8020-5898-1 (bound)   ISBN 0-8020-6837-5 (pbk.)

1. France – History – Revolution, 1789–1799 – Women.
2. Women in public life – France – History – 18th century.
3. Women revolutionaries – France – History – 18th century.
4. France – History – 1789–1815.
I. Title.   II. Series.

DC158.8.H84 1992   944.04'082   C91-095142-X

for Clare, sparring partner and alter ego
in memory of a shared experience

Contents

Foreword   ix

Preface   xv

CHAPTER ONE
Women and Politics
1

CHAPTER TWO
Poverty and Charity: Revolutionary Mythology and
Real Women
51

CHAPTER THREE
In Search of Counter-Revolutionary Women
89

CHAPTER FOUR
Epilogue. The Legacy: Myth and Memory
131

Notes   155

Select Bibliography   179

Index   198

Foreword

The historian whose name this lecture series honours, Donald Creighton, was born in 1902 and died in 1979. Most of his long and productive life was spent in and around the Department of History at the University of Toronto. He was first an undergraduate here, at Victoria College, and then, after a stint at Balliol College, Oxford, he joined the Department as a Lecturer in 1927. There followed forty-four years during which he served a five-year term as Head of the Department, was President of the Canadian Historical Association, won almost every literary award available to a historian in Canada, and by the end of his career he had become a University Professor, the highest honour this University can bestow on its faculty.

On his death, a group of his friends and former students formed a committee whose purpose was to create a fund which would sustain a lecture or symposium series in Donald Creighton's name. The first lecturer in this series was William H. McNeil, whose three lectures on *Polyethnicity and National Unity in World History* were delivered in 1985 and published by the University of Toronto Press in 1986. Two years later Maurice Careless delivered the second in the Donald Creighton Lecture series, and his lectures, *Frontier and Metropolis: Regions, Cities, and Identities in Canada before 1914*, were published in 1989. The lectures that follow are the third in this distinguished lectureship.

From the early thirties, when he started writing history in earnest, until the mid-sixties, Donald Creighton produced remarkable economic, political, and biographical works that were shaped by a distinctive national vision and inspired a generation of younger scholars. The *Commercial Empire of The St Lawrence, British North America at Confederation, Dominion of the North,* and his two-volume biography of Sir John A. Macdonald are some of the works that made Creighton a household name and gave early shape to the study of Canadian history as an academic discipline.

Donald Creighton was not without critics in his lifetime nor has criticism been silenced since his death. What cannot be denied, however, is that Donald Creighton succeeded in doing what most historians can only aspire to: he created the paradigms and shaped his discipline for more than a generation. Not everyone has accepted his vision of this country's past – or of its future – but none can ignore it.

Donald Creighton was, of course, a historian of Canada. Perhaps what everyone does not know is that he began his academic career as a historian of the French Revolution. He not only taught courses in modern Eu-

ropean history in the late twenties, he also began research in eighteenth-century French history. As Carl
Berger has reminded us, Donald Creighton spent the
summer of 1928 at the Sorbonne, carrying out research
under the supervision of the great socialist historian
Albert Mathiez. It was only the virtual impossibility of
spending time in French archives that persuaded him
of the prudence of writing history that could be re-
searched closer to home. Had the Social Sciences and
Humanities Research Council of Canada existed in 1928
as it does today, who can say what might have been
its effect on the writing and making of Canadian history – and on the writing of the history of pre-revo-
lutionary France.

Perhaps we don't know what kind of historian he
might have become with modern research grant support, but we do know that Donald Creighton would
have been pleased that the third lecturer in the series
established to honour him, Professor Olwen Hufton,
is a historian who is in the midst of a career in the area
of his first academic love.

Professor Hufton studied for her PhD at the University of London under the direction of Alfred Cobban. She spent very little time turning her thesis into
her first book, *Bayeux in the Late Eighteenth Century: A
Social Study*, published in 1967. This was an investi-
gation of the social structure of a middle-sized French
administrative and ecclesiastical town in the generation
preceding the French Revolution, with a view to seeing
how its inhabitants 'lived under the old regime and
what effects the Revolution had on their livelihood.'
In her first book, Professor Hufton paid considerable
attention to the poor, though, of course, she also concerned herself with the noblesse, the bourgeoisie, and

especially the clergy in that highly ecclesiastical urban centre.

Her interest in the poor, that lowest 20 per cent of the population of Bayeux who relied on 'outside relief' to sustain their unbelievably low standard of living, led her to a more systematic study of this social group. In 1974 she published her second book, *The Poor of Eighteenth-Century France*. After an exhaustive study of diffuse, scattered, and difficult sources she answered the question how vast numbers of people without visible means of support survive and procreate by observing that they did so 'by their own efforts, devious, ugly, cruel, and dishonest as these might be.'

Perhaps to cheer herself up after spending over a decade with the abjectly impoverished, and perhaps to prove that she could write what some might still regard as real history, i.e. political history, Professor Hufton published her third book in 1980, *Europe: Privilege and Protest, 1730–1789*. This was as sharply argued and highly successful attempt to place the French Revolution in its broader European context.

In the 1980s Professor Hufton's academic life changed in two ways. First she became part of the English brain drain by forsaking the University of Reading, where she had become Professor of History, for the greener pastures of Harvard University. Second, and more relevant to readers of this volume of lectures, she turned her attention to the study of women. She has for a number of years been publishing articles and chapters that will become her next book, one that is tentatively entitled the 'Making of the European Woman.' This book is scheduled to be published in the next year or two, and may well have been already completed had she not been gracious enough to accept our invitation

to deliver the third in the Donald G. Creighton Lecture
series in October 1989.

Michael G. Finlayson
Chair, Department of History
University of Toronto
April 1991

Preface

These lectures originated as a series in memory of the late Donald Creighton, someone I knew only through his international reputation as a historian of Canada, but who, I was delighted to learn, almost became a historian of France. That he did not do so reflected the hardness and unsettled nature of the times in which he started graduate study. I was also told that he had a deep appreciation of Zola and so on a double account I think he might have approved of both the context and the content of these lectures. They were given in October 1989 and served as a tribute to the bicentenary of the French Revolution, and the dramatis personae of at least two of the lectures were the ancestors of Zola's people. The spirit of *Germinal* is ever pervasive.

During my stay in Toronto, I much enjoyed the hospitality of the Creighton family and of the history department under the benign aegis of Michael Finlayson. It was warming to talk to graduate students, to catch up on developments in women's history where Toronto is a pioneer, and to talk to my old and treasured friends David Higgs and Bill Callahan.

I feel especially grateful for an occasion which made me commit to paper my thoughts on a topic which has preoccupied me for longer than I care to think. My first tentative steps in this field were taken more than twenty years ago when the world was much younger and revolutions, in some circles at least, were regarded as necessary, desirable, and perhaps even fun. I was asked in the autumn of 1968 by the history society of Balliol College, Oxford, to contribute to a series called 'Revolutions' a paper on women in the French Revolution. Although the author of an urban monograph, I had not really considered this topic before, though my notes soon demonstrated that I did not lack material. The series included illustrous names like Christopher Hill, Edward Thompson, and George Rudé and my presence with this distinguished team – largely, I think, due to the suggestion of Richard Cobb, who, as I recall, forgot to come until ten minutes before the end – reflected the dearth of competition for the task. What I remember most clearly was the feeling amongst the radical young that there must be a gender topic if the series was to be truly revolutionary. These young men, for Balliol had yet to become mixed, took me out to dinner before the event, and a member of the society, Bernard Wasserstein, now Professor of History at Brandeis and author of a best-selling work on the spy Trebbich Lincoln, informed me that, so far, I was the only invitee who had both turned up and proposed to address the allotted topic. The talk seemed to gratify the audience and news that Hufton had a paper on women in the Revolution got around. I dined out on it all the next winter as the guest of student history societies. I sent it to *Past and Present* in late May and then gave birth to a child in October whilst it mouldered on Trevor Aston's desk.

Once in print, the piece laid the foundation of a large number of transatlantic contacts of which the most immediate was Natalie Davis. We had never met but at that time she and Jill Conway were launching a course on the history of women in Toronto and were compiling a pioneer bibliography. She wrote to me for suggestions of works on France and the Revolution. I passed on all I had. That was how the first steps were taken by teachers in the field. We networked with those we had never even met.

Since those days, the corpus of work on women and their past has burgeoned beyond belief and for the bicentenary there were several works dedicated specifically to women in the French Revolution.[1] It is not my intention to replicate these works or even summarize them and although many more details now exist, I would not even seek to remould my initial essay. I think I got right what I set out to accomplish. Rather, I want to take an opportunity to examine a number of issues more closely with a view not merely to proving that women were there and hence had a revolution as well, but that their responses transformed and modified the entire history of the period 1789–1815.

As a historian, and I make no apologies, I have always been preoccupied with the business of survival in the past and with perceptions and convictions (*mentalités*) which explain why people responded to events the way they did. As an empiricist I also confess to a sense of discomfort with some of the grand claims about

the changing nature of women's lives which have
surfaced during the bicentennial year when political
discourse became the sovereign preoccupation. Pronouncements about women encapsulated in specific
texts issuing from individual or eclectic groups of men
or women have been used as a commentary on the
entire sex, and a generic woman or a version of womanhood with a questionable relationship to any real
woman or women has been constructed. We have been
asked to view the Revolution as a factor accelerating
the banishment of women into the home, the private
sphere, and quite extraordinary claims about the 'freedom' and 'public presence' of the 'eighteenth-century
woman' have been made in contrast to the domestic
bondage of 'nineteenth-century woman' on the flim-
siest of evidence. A generic, theoretical woman has
emerged, Phoenix-like, from the experience of a dozen
salonnières, a couple of courtesans – to represent public
woman – from the writings of the philosophes and a
handful of women writers, to include some of the earliest women writers with a discernible feminist agenda
such as Olympe de Gouges and Mary Wollstonecraft.[2]
Such an exercise should not be confused with the actual
experience of real women. We should, as historians, be
conscious of the demarcation between theory and what
actually happened as well as prepared to recognize that
theories could play a part in policies and the subsequent
interpretation of events.

The first historian to seek to write a gendered history
of the French Revolution was Jules Michelet. He too
sought to distil the women who lived during the Revolution into a single generic woman. Michelet was a
professor at the Collège de France and in many ways

a historian for our times since he drew upon memory, both first- and second-hand, of women and men. He had himself worked for a decade or more in the archives. He discerned, as indeed any serious historian who spends time in the records must do, that two issues, bread and religion, were those where the presence of women could be detected. Michelet proceeded to extrapolate from this evidence a different perception of the Revolution when seen by 'women' from the view of 'men.' He compounded the woman of the bread riot with the counter-revolutionary woman of the Vendée and presented the involvement of women in the Revolution as a serial disaster. In *Les Femmes de la Révolution* (Paris 1854), Michelet examined the role of women from the evidence of the great events. At first he admired their dynamism, their spontaneity, and their sensibility. Under his eloquent pen, women become privileged victims whose contact with daily needs, hunger, disease, and family responsibility made them impulsive but courageous instigators of revolt and, in his view, particularly laudatory ones because their violent behaviour was minimal. The October Days were hence 'naïve,' 'spontaneous,' 'determined by needs,' and 'shed no blood'. However, the volatility of women, their 'excessive sensibility,' their 'credulity,' and their proneness to heed priests made them and their influence ultimately fatal to the forward movement of the Revolution. Michelet makes women and sensibility equivalent and this equivalence becomes for him the explanation for the incompatibility of (generic) woman with the Revolution. For him, the Revolution represented the triumph of reason and this attribute is interpreted as male. Ultimately the history of the Revolution in the hands of Michelet is one wherein reason is undermined by sensibility. Put crudely, it is a victory of a female over a male attribute.

Michelet's eloquence, his learning, and the power of his imagination should not be underestimated. His section on the Vendée included an imagined bedroom scene in which a patriotic husband prepared to accept the logic of revolutionary legislation is denied sleep by a nagging wife who is concerned about the fate of the priest and her eternal soul.[3] Whilst obviously transcending the limits of his evidence and relying upon creative intuition, Michelet concedes to women the control of a subversive home, a political unit which ultimately destroys the fabric of the revolutionary state. Michelet's housewife also controls the purse-strings and starves the state of its lawful taxes.

No one, and Michelet paid for doing so in professional terms, has ever exceeded the claims he made for the influence of women on the French Revolution. Whether or not one agrees with the inferences he draws, the questions he asks about differing perceptions of the Revolution by men and women remain central. His conclusions were integrated, sometimes with a conspicuous lack of subtlety, into both the republican and the socialist historiographical tradition. Arguably, Mathiez best encapsulated the approach of a whole three-quarters of a century of socialist writing when he argued that women turned from the *fanatisme de leurs clubs* to the *fanatisme de leurs prêtres*.[4] Again, he managed to convey the idea of a simple female model characterized by excess. He was particularly devoted to Robespierre and to justifying the phenomenon of Terror.[5] Robespierre or the government of which he was a part had, in the fall of 1793, closed the women's political clubs (see below) and the incident provided Mathiez with the appropriate tone for dismissing the influence of women on politics. A fervent anticlerical, he also summarized much of the fear felt by the republicans of the Third Republic about the influence of religion on women. The political struggles surrounding attempts to laicize the state and the resistance in certain areas to the demolition of Catholic social services fostered and perpetuated the fear that clerical influence was perpetuated through women. The notion of woman as a political and religious fanatic which served as the ongoing justification in many quarters for denying women the vote drew upon the experience of the first French Revolution as a cautionary tale. Women, given the chance, would undermine anything savouring of political radicalism.

The simple evolutionary view of a revolutionary woman – bread rioter, *clubiste, dévôte* – is seductively persuasive. The records themselves show that when we look for women they were indeed defenders of the bread basket; some were also members of political clubs and many certainly worked for the restoration of Catholic worship in France. But were they the same women? Was there any relationship between them? Is the destructive and far from impassive female force that the republican and socialist tradition insisted helped to undermine the ideals of the Revolution and ultimately the Revolution itself an accurate representation of all or even a majority of women in the context of the Revolution? If the answer to this question should be yes, were the women really the product of sensibility (as Michelet said) or of stupidity (as Mathiez implied) which flouted pure masculine reason? If the answer should be no, why might the issues have been formulated in these terms?

When I first read Elsa Morante's *History* (London 1978), a novel about the survival process of a schoolteacher, the mother of two sons, in Mussolini's Italy, I was consumed with a mixture of admiration and envy. It is a work which every historian should read. I was subsumed by the desire to write a similar account of a working woman in the context of the French Revolution. She would be a textile worker or perhaps a peasant woman, certainly a mother of three without a man to support her. One of her sons, like Morante's adolescent, would be fired by revolutionary idealism. He would help break up statues and would ransack chateaux, as a typical vandalistic adolescent. He would want to fight for his country but once at the front, disillusionment would gradually set in. He would take to the hills as a deserter, a partisan of a sort, and he would evolve as a political cynic. His mother, would watch the course of events with some trepidation. She would know all about the promises of politicians but also about food queues, shortages, struggling to provide milk and basic necessities for two infants in the context of war. Condemned to a remorseless and seemingly endless struggle for mere basic survival, she would know hunger and pain and cold. She might be one of the allegedly numerous rape victims of the *armées révolutionnaires*. Certainly, like the Dutch women in the closing months of the Second World War and many of her compatriots in 1796 she would experience amenorrhoea. Her body would be a personal metering device for the record of the Revolution. And the end of all her efforts might be the death of her children as their resistance to disease was lowered by malnutrition. Then, perhaps, she would sink to her knees and reach for her rosary beads. Or would she?

The problem was that although dearth, disease, death, and devotion are abundantly documented, to construct a single, continuous experience of a working woman in the Revolution exceeds the evidence. The section of the population from which such a woman came has left relatively little continuous testimony. Sixty-five per cent of women on the eve of the Revolution could not write their own names. The historian must depend, as Michelet did, on administrative sources, above all police records, municipal registers, reports of national agents – a far from neutral source – and scattered information in provincial archives such as the series Lx (*Assistance*). These might be given some further embellishment by the quantitative information of censuses and the *état civil*, the kind of information that would permit glimpses of the behaviour of certain women at certain times but no single continuous saga.

I have elected therefore to remain within the limits set by the evidence and to pursue, without assuming a relationship between any of them, the experience of certain groups or kinds of women. I have several aims but my overriding concern is to examine aspects of the total record and to explain why certain groups of women behaved the way they did and the consequences of their actions for the history of the Revolution and indeed for the history of France. Where appropriate I shall try to fit the rhetoric issuing from the politicians on womanhood into context and explain how such pronouncements were prompted by particular experiences and could have influence on some women's lives.

I do not claim to be writing a general history of women in the Revolution for I believe the topic to be too vast and too diffuse. Rather, like Virginia Woolf with three guineas to spend, I shall elect three issues to validate my purpose. I shall take three issues of primary concern. My first chapter will concentrate on Paris and I will examine the history of the crowd and the politics of popular sovereignty. The second is designed to explore the relationship between enlightenment ideas and revolutionary reform policy to demonstrate why gender attitudes and an understanding of gender roles transform our understanding of what happened and why the reform policy went wrong. Thirdly, I shall leave Paris for the provinces and by looking at gender roles in the counter-revolution seek to convey how it was possible for women to subvert the Revolution in the home and on the domestic front. I shall argue that in innumerable small and insidious ways some groups of women in particular French villages did conduct a guerrilla warfare against revolutionary ideals and won. Moreover, some groups of women, as teachers and mothers, may well have controlled the presentation of the Revolution to the succeeding generations. Was it grandmother or grandfather who instructed the generation of 1848 to beware of the wild men of Paris? Finally, in the epilogue, I shall draw some conclusions and point to generalities and re-examine Michelet's legacy. A recurrent theme of the work will be the limits of citizenship or the application of that term when applied to women. I do not think I am writing a three-act tragedy so much as an essay in misunderstanding or a historical cautionary tale.

Before I embark, I should like to acknowledge two debts

in my historical formation. The first is to Alfred Cobban who taught me my *métier* and so fixed my destiny in my undergraduate and graduate classes at University College, London. Cobban was a very special person as teacher, scholar, and human being. He had an unerring talent for spotting the flaws in an argument. I was the fortunate recipient of the lectures which were to form the basis of *In Search of Humanity* (London 1960) and, later, *The Social Interpretation of the French Revolution* (Cambridge 1964). The second was intended as a challenge to many of the then prevalent orthodoxies and, when published, sparked off a great deal of hostility amongst a scholarly community in which a Marxist interpretation of the Revolution predominated. Yet 1989 has witnessed Cobban's vindication. In Ran Halevi's words, 'Cobban opened up the discourse and made it possible for the two sides to talk to each other.'[6] Certainly, his work anticipated many of the discussions of the bicentenary.

I remember Cobban most for two things. He told me as an undergraduate that he thought me a social historian in the making and, although I was no political theorist, infused me with an enthusiasm for the ideals of the Enlightenment. He exulted in the way fixed ideas which were centuries old disintegrated under the interrogation of a set of probing minds who believed they applied a purely rationalistic spirit. He loved argument and I treasure discussions with him which tested the ideas of the philosophers against reality. Some of the ideas in the second chapter took shape in this way.

My other intellectual debt must be to Richard Cobb. More than any other historian he, in his works on the Revolution, questioned the gap between language and reality, and his point of departure was that all ambitious men could be liars under duress and say what their superiors wanted to hear. Hating all forms of pontificating authority and excited by the collapse of central control during the directorial period, Richard Cobb found a kind of spiritual home in the anarchy of 1796–1801. His favourite people were those who could survive where lack of order reigned. To him I dedicate my counter-revolutionary women.

Finally, I wrote the Creighton lectures in the immensely stimulating and nurturing atmosphere of the Minda de Gunzburg Center for European Studies at Harvard. My office lies between those of Stanley Hoffman and Patrice Higonnet, two esteemed new friends, whilst upstairs on the fourth floor are, an old and treasured one, Simon Schama, and a fellow historian of women and religion, Caroline Ford. Their warmth has enriched my stay in Cambridge and Simon will not be surprised to find in my *citoyennes* a different kind of view, a more modest but alternative chronicle of the Revolution.

Olwen Hufton
Cambridge 1991

CHAPTER ONE

Women and Politics

Women and Politics

When the politicians of the Constituent Assembly debated the critical issue of who should possess the suffrage in the new France and hence gave practical
expression to the notion of equality, they excluded three
types of people. The first were the poor, or more specifically those who did not pay a tax equivalent to the
proceeds from three days' labour. The second were
servants, because their impartiality could not be guaranteed, and the third exclusion was that of women.
Much debate focused on the first two exemptions and
indeed Robespierre made his political reputation in a
moving speech which insisted that citizenship belonged to all men. The last omission went totally un-
challenged. The rights of man were not the rights of

mankind and the equality was that of the economically sufficient male able to defend himself in the free market economy. If the Constituents had a view of women (and that they did was to surface in subsequent debates on female religious and the issue of poverty), it was straight out of *Emile* and the Enlightenment.

According to this view, women were not political animals. Nature locked them in the private sphere. The male citizen was seen as active with a destiny that involved service to *la nation*. Public man, like David's *Horatii* in the most reproduced image of fraternal revolutionary *Zeitgeist*, was prepared to lay down his life in defence of republican values. His wife's only task was to produce and nurture citizens who would count themselves honoured to die for the Republic of Virtue. *Voilà la citoyenne*. After four sections dedicated to the rearing of the ideal citizen in an environment free from prejudice, wherein he allows Emile to give free rein to his questioning mind, to leave the nest and to scatter his wild oats at will, Rousseau arrives at the moment when the ideal citizen must be given an ideal wife. Enter Sophie. Few word are expended on the rearing of our hero's mate. She exists merely to please her husband and to nurture his legitimate offspring, to perpetuate his property. To make her content with this role and to curtail her natural coquetry and guile, Sophie must be educated in the art of pleasing and to appreciate the values of chastity. She cannot roam free if Emile is to rest quiet about the legitimacy of his children. Sophie must stay home, the only fit place for the virtuous – that is, according to contemporary ideas, the chaste – woman. The Sophie model will surface here and there in the discourse of the Revolution. She is always in the politicians' intellectual baggage, to be exposed when the going gets rough; but she can easily be stored away in the attic. She is, however, something of a peacetime ideal. In the context of the Revolution she is occasionally transformed into, or even blended with Cornelia, mother of the Gracchi, the implacable Roman matron whose iron will transmitted to her sons through iron milk transformed them into instant heroes and whose vision of the state allowed her to triumph over grief when they were slain.

So much for the rhetoric. In July 1789, those to be denied citizenship stormed the Bastille and in October brought the king to Paris and established French political life in the capital. These two events achieved momentous political change. The first ensured the continuation of the Constituent Assembly and the second sought to resolve two perennial problems: the isolation of the king in a corrupt court where his wife and family could bend his ear and potentially reverse the Revolution, and the absence from the capital of the locus of political power. As Robert Darnton recently reminded us, we do not have a history of public opinion on the eve of the Revolution. What we know is that for many, bread was politics, and that the people identified the king as the only force capable of resolving the problem of the grain supply in the capital. In short, twice in 1789, those who were denied citizenship intervened in political life and their capacity to bring about change was troubling to the politicians. The people were seen as intrinsically good, but their capacity to intrude and effect change by force of numbers disquieted those who in the autumn of 1789 sat debating the merits of limiting the suffrage to the modestly affluent – those who did not have to worry about the contents of the bread bin.

The crowd the politicians feared was not lacking a gender dimension. The October Days were women's days and those of germinal and prairial in the year III were to be the same. These days had distinct attributes though a great deal in common with each other.

However, while historians have acknowledged the presence of women, they have hardly touched upon the full implications of that presence and the goals they sought to achieve. It is not that the crowd has been neglected since George Rudé produced his trail-blazing study in 1959.[1] Its legitimizing notions have been pursued by Thompson and its symbolic ritualism has provided a feast for Geerz and Lévi-Strauss, etc.[2] Very recently, Colin Lucas has carried our understanding still further by emphasizing continuity and tradition, as well as radical points of departure, within the revolutionary crowd.[3] We now know better than to think of a 'simple' crowd but must give further definition. There are reactive and pre-emptive crowds, panic crowds, festive crowds, theatre crowds, radical crowds, orchestrated crowds, purposive crowds, revolutionary crowds (those who gather to carry the Revolution forward) and the subcategorization does not stop.[4]

Yet, and with homage made to Natalie Davis, the gendered crowd has not had much of a look in. By Rudé, women are treated, somewhat dismissively, as only involved in food riots or those *journées* where food was a critical issue. Women in this work might be said only to think with their stomachs. This could, however, be fairly described as a rather limited interpretation, especially given the consequences of the October Days. However, Rudé did include women, if somewhat perfunctorily, in his pioneering work. They exist too in the pages of Cobb and Tønnesson,[5] though they have had

to await Dominique Godineau's study of germinal/
prairial to get extensive consideration. I would argue,
however, that to understand the role of the gendered
crowd between 1789 and 1795 we need to review it as
a continuum with distinctive characteristics. It is as
members of such a crowd that the women who were
denied citizenship impinge most conspicuously upon
the high history of the French Revolution.

Not many women were present at the storming of the
Bastille. We are told by one reliable observer that as
the victorious crowd poured up the rue Saint Antoine,
the parish from which 70 per cent of the participants
came, its prisoners in tow, 'an inconceivable number
of women, children and old people ... seemed to burst
out of the houses, crying "there they are, the villains,
we've got them."[6]
  The glory was clearly shared, yet the women had
remained behind closed doors. Why? Was it because
there was a strong possibility that shots would be ex-
changed? Was confronting the guards in an arsenal
interpreted as men's work? I think we should hold this
possibility in mind. Three months later, the conditions
were quite different. Let us reconstruct what happened
as faithfully as we can from evidence which is frequently partial and contradictory.[7]

At dawn, on Monday, 5 October, a group of between
eight hundred and two thousand women converged –
not par hazard – on the Hôtel de Ville, forced the doors,
and rushed inside. They then proceeded to throw out
the men who had helped them to force the door and
denied any of them entry. Then they ransacked the
place for arms and found a number of pikes though

no ammunition. They seized as many papers and files as they could lay their hands on and prepared to make a huge bonfire of them in the hall, claiming that they contained nothing which would help them to get a better supply of bread. They were, according to one rendering, dissuaded from this by Maillard, a member of the National Guard, brother to a petty official at the Hôtel de Ville and, most pertinently, one of the *vainqueurs de la Bastille* and hence someone they trusted.[8] Then either they persuaded him to lead them in their march to Versailles or, some versions say, he offered to go with them to keep an eye on them (but this was not his testimony). Whatever the agreement between Maillard and the women it also involved taking two cannons with them though they had no ammunition. Then the women set off for another rendezvous. Some went to the Invalides to see if any ammunition could be found, and the rest went home to round up as many women as they could. Children went around the parish of Saint Eustache with a bugle and a bell. In this way the number of women was doubled or perhaps even trebled. The least reliable part of the evidence pertains to numbers.[9] There was a general rendezvous at the Place Louis XV and the women who gathered carried brooms and kitchen tools. Very few had pikes. It was almost afternoon before they set off with eight drummers at their head and with Maillard out front. They were followed several hours later by the National Guard headed by Lafayette, who, according to some accounts, did not want to go either because he feared what might happen in his absence in the capital or because he thought that the Guard might make the women's protest more dangerous. In some interpretations, he cedes to pressure from the Guard to express to the monarchy their outrage at the conduct of the Flanders regiment. Later still, after work, groups of men set off.

The women chanted and sang in festive mood about what they were going to do at Versailles. En route and in a persistent drizzle they picked up more women. There may have been some coercion involved but there was no lack of opportunity for the coerced to fall away. The crowd was far from unified. Some groups became angry, when at Sèvres, Maillard encountered opposition from shopkeepers over the supply of refreshments but without serious incident, and although this event has been used to imply that the women in question were *bacchantes*, the amount of wine involved was very small, so small, in fact, that the quantity serves as evidence for those who wish to reduce the size of the crowd of women who went on that day.[10]

They arrived in Versailles around five o'clock, and after some discussion about their first move they took themselves to the National Assembly where some filled the tribunes; some remained outside and some looked for a place to camp. The weather was bad and the women were already soaked. Some of them removed their outer clothing and spread it out to dry in the assembly hall.

The Assembly had been warned to expect their arrival. It was in course of debating the issue of compensation for feudal rights, and the women became impatient. This was not business they deemed relevant. They were granted permission to deliver a petition and Maillard was their spokesman. The petition was a complaint in highly personalized terms about speculation in the grain trade. They said that they wanted an audience with the king. The occasion was initially quite orderly though it became rowdier as the women got used to their surroundings and they directed particularly offensive remarks towards the clergy who tried to bring them to order. *A bas les calotins*. Both the bishop of Langres and the Abbé Grégoire suffered particularly smarting insults. The delegation of about twelve,[11] including a seventeen-year-old girl named Louise Chabry, was accompanied to the palace to see the king around seven o'clock. She is said to have mouthed the words 'du pain' and to have fallen in a breathless faint at the feet of the king (a nice damsel in distress touch but, one feels, one more suitable for Louis xv) and the king promised to see to it that the city was adequately provisioned.

The delegation returned and reported to the women and the majority were totally dissatisfied. What guarantees had the monarch offered? Had the delegation got anything in writing? The fainting seventeen-year-old was accused of accepting bribes and some accounts, though the least reliable, say that an attempt was made to hang her. Michelet strenuously denies this.[12] However, the women were certainly angry. If they went back to Paris with no more than promises, how was their situation improved? The king was still locked in the court with his whore of a wife.

The few who thought they had done well enough went back home. Maillard took the opportunity to leave as well. The women were now split into groups. Many went back to the Assembly, which came to resemble an unruly camp. Women occupied the president's chair and imitated the proceedings in the midst of the drying clothes. The politicians, or at least some of them, decided they must carry on and continued in desultory fashion. Some of the women slept on the Assembly benches. Other invaded the Hôtel de la Surintendance

and ministerial offices which gave them shelter from
what was now driving rain. Inside the château, the king
and his advisers were absorbed in discussion. The
women's presence was disconcerting and there was
news that a larger crowd was on the way. The flight
of the royal family was discussed, but the king was not
convinced of the need. By ten in the evening, news
came to the Assembly that the king had accepted the
constitution with its limitations on royal sovereignty.
The women in the hall were not sure how this benefited
them. By ten o'clock the National Guard arrived and
Lafayette told the king that order and his personal safety
could only be guaranteed if he and his family came to
the capital. The king would not agree. In the small
hours the men arrived and in the semi-darkness the
mood became uglier. Some of the crowd broke into the
palace and tried to force entry to the queen's bed-
chamber. In the confrontation, two of the royal body-
guards were slain (not by women). At this stage of the
mêlée the role of the women had conspicuously di-
minished though it is at this juncture that we hear from
the more royalist accounts of men dressed up as women.
The National Guard intervened and when order had
been restored the king appeared publicly on the bal-
cony before perhaps as many as ten thousand people.
He promised bread and, overwhelmed by the shouting,
finally agreed to go back to the capital.

It was a triumphal procession. Mercier says it was
twenty thousand strong by the time it got to the Tuil-
eries, though again estimates of the numbers are not
to be trusted.

The procession must have been an extraordinary
sight. It was preceded by the heads of the two dead
guards carried on poles. The women linked arms with

the National Guard and bedecked them and the cannon with laurel leaves. Loaves of bread were carried on staves. Much could be read into these symbols of peace and plenty. The king, his family, and their servants were in carriages. The king's bodyguard followed and there were wagons containing flour from the king's store. It was, to all accounts, an extraordinarily moving, if damp, rentrée. The rain did not cease to fall. The people, however, were triumphant and the credit for the event was given entirely to the women. Michelet echoed contemporaries when he said that the men took the Bastille and the women took the king.

Let us now seek to explain some of the features of this extraordinary event. Why did the women go? Why the relay women, guards, men?

The background to this *journée* was indeed the inadequacy of bread supplies and their continuing high price, but it also included growing dissatisfaction with the role of government and with the king in particular. The monarch's reluctance to register the suspensive veto and hence the new constitution and the legislation involving feudal rights and the reported incident in which the king's guard entertained the Flander's regiment and allegedly spurned the revolutionary cockade and donned ones of black (Hapsburg) and white (Bourbon), reverberated around the capital in broadside pamphlet and print. The importation of the regiment implied that the king did not trust his personal safety to the National Guard and their behaviour in the presence of the royal family, even if they did not trample the revolutionary colours underfoot, was indiscreet and their drunken toasts of personal loyalty to the monarch were liable to misinterpretation.[13]

The orators of the Palais Royale had a field-day with

the story. It presented the royal family, whose presence was seen as an endorsement of the guards' conduct, in the worst possible light. An important part of the political situation for the working population, however, was the question of provisioning the people – a hot political issue – and the sense of frustration that, even after the storming of the Bastille and the lynching of the Intendant of Paris and the food purveyors, nothing that was being done was having real effect. It is difficult to explain why prices did not fall in the aftermath of the harvest as they usually did. Reasons such as the sluggishness of the grinding mills as a result of prolonged drought failed to convince as the weather in the fall turned distinctly wet. An alternative meteorological reason proffered, and tried again in 1794, was the lack of wind to turn windmills. These were reasons which the people had heard many times before and which failed to sway them.

Perhaps the most convincing explanation is that the usual glut of grain on the market as peasants sold in order to pay seigneurial and royal taxes simply did not occur in 1789 as the peasantry for the first time were in no hurry to sell. Every farmer knew enough to hold on until the last possible moment to see if prices would rise.[14] The delay, however, mystified the city dweller. Why didn't something happen? From September, a people's march to Versailles to remonstrate with the king had been mooted and was, according to several commentators, openly discussed in Paris but there is no evidence to suggest that this was a uniquely female preoccupation. In the days before the forcing of the Hôtel de Ville we hear that groups of women accused the men of hanging back – 'les hommes traînent ... les hommes sont des lâches ... Demain des choses iront

mieux: nous nous mettrons à la tête des affaires.'[15]
Such accusations, followed by the willingness of women
to act in default of male action, remind us of a legal
situation in which an insulted woman whose husband
failed to defend her before the appropriate lawcourt
was seen as justified in initiating her own suit and in
so doing dishonoured her partner for his failure to act.
The women who went to the Hôtel de Ville, a rendezvous previously organized, wanted action. They
were pre-empting a situation. All wanted bread out of
the monarchy and some, perhaps, though one cannot
be sure, thought that this would be best guaranteed by
the revivification of politics which would result from
severing the chief baker from the court and placing
him amongst his people. Perhaps those commentators
who said that the women were opening up the situation
or trying to force their way out of an impasse got their
analysis right.

Yet why keep the men out of the Hôtel de Ville? Because, I think, the women were intent upon a particular
kind of demonstration which the men might have ruined,
a demonstration which was non-violent or of limited
violence. They, or some of them, did carry pikes, and
they insisted that they should take the cannon but they
had little, if any, ammunition. They placed a soldier at
their head. They wanted to look serious and indicate
that if their peaceful proposals were not accepted a
different kind of demonstration might follow. Their
weapons were symbolic. It is seriously to be doubted
whether any of the woman present could have fired a
cannon but that piece of equipment gave them a mil-
itaristic overtone.

The destruction, or attempted destruction of papers
in the Hôtel de Ville, stormed to demonstrate anger at

the failure of Bailly and the Commune to provide the
people with bread, to secure the equipment and the
military leadership, and to express some contempt for
the inefficacy of a male government which put words
before deeds, expressed a certain impatience with the
futility of bureaucracy – men's work. The women left
the living quarters of the lieutenant de police where
his wife was said to be sleeping – though it seems
improbable in light of the noise – untouched, thus re-
specting a woman's home. They had much less respect
for Marie Antoinette's home but she was to all accounts
an unvirtuous wife. They then proceeded to what they
saw as the seat of power. Were they politically innocent? What is innocent about starting at the top and
surely the truly desperate have the best right to start
at the top? There was in many cases here a re-enact-
ment of a traditional pattern. Women in the hard winter
of 1708–9 had marched to Versailles to implore Louis
XIV to take action to end a famine and to stop the war.
The *poissardes* – market women – had had an open line
to the monarchy which Maria Leczinska, wife to the
playboy king, Louis XV, and one of the most popular
queens of France, had encouraged. Maria Leczinska's
reputation amongst ordinary Parisian women rose in
inverse proportion to her lecherous husband's unpop-
ularity. The young Marie Antoinette had been an early
target of the fishwives' tongues because of her failure
to get pregnant. Unlike her grandmother-in-law she did
not encourage the presence of the *poissardes*. They saw
the queen as a bad wife and a bad mother; *Madame
Déficit, Madame Véto.*[16] Marie Antoinette had the reputation of holding the king back from the Revolution
and was suspected to be an agent of backlash. Hence
the stories about the behaviour of the Flander's regi-

ment in the royal presence and their disrespect for the revolutionary cockade seemed perfectly plausible. To adopt Bourbon and Habsburg colours was to remind Paris of the unpopular connections of the queen.

There was no political ignorance in the verbal attack the women made on the clergy in the Assembly for the clergy had staunchly opposed the reduction of the monarchy's power through the veto. But did they intend to bring the king to Paris? Several observers testified to this effect in the admittedly very dubious Procédure Criminelle but the most obvious evidence is the purely circumstantial. Most of the women did not leave Versailles after the unsatisfactory audience with the king. They were furious that their efforts, so far successful, had met with a check. They had no guarantees that the bread would be delivered. Perhaps, and this is only speculation, more would have settled for a written undertaking from the monarchy that grain would be forthcoming. In the event, they turned their fury on the delegation which had seen the king and then split up to find shelter and a camp until the men arrived. The event had now to move on into another phase in which they ceded the initiative to the men. Maillard perhaps sensed this and decided to leave so as to avoid compromising himself in violence. It was a strategic exit. From this point, the likelihood of armed conflict, or at least a menacing confrontation between the king's guards at Versailles and the populace, was to be anticipated.

The crowd of women was in all ways a purposive and a revolutionary crowd in Lefebvre's sense even though there may not have been total consensus among the different parts about how far they should go. It was also a reactive crowd in the sense that it perceived the need to defend the Revolution from aristocrats and clerics. Was it a spontaneous crowd? Were the women tutored in what to do? Were they the tools of political intriguers?

No one, however hard they have tried, has yet found evidence that the initial crowd of women was 'set up.' Some royalist and clerical accounts allude to 'women in white dresses' who were thus defined as something other than women of the people and possible pay-masters in the service of an ambitious aristocrat like the Duke of Orleans. The evidence for this, however, is flimsy.[17] The constant theme is the refrain of hunger, which is hardly trivial, and of the men's cowardice in hanging back. The women were not, however, pre-pared to take on the royal bodyguard without the re-inforcement of their menfolk. They opened up the situation. They demonstrated how far a peaceful, if intimidatingly large, demonstration could go and then, as it were, handed over the responsibility.

Contemporaries did not hesitate to attribute the Oc-tober Days to women in the way that many subsequent historians tried to do. The bookseller Hardy who wit-nessed the return to Paris thought that he saw a man dressed as a woman and when the invasion of the château occurred a royalist commentator was of the same opinion but such evidence does not convert the October Days into a transvestite triumph.[18] Victorian historians liked this interpretation because it accorded with their view of woman as an apolitical animal.[19] Another favoured nineteenth-century interpretation was that the men chose the women because their hun-ger cries were shriller. Burke, inevitably, but also Car-lyle and Taine converted the active women into *la lie du peuple*, prostitutes in large part, but this does not accord with the evidence. Many of the women were market women, wives of artisans and tradeswomen. It seems, and this is corroborated by the later women's *journées*, that the women were either over fifty or very young. It is a defining characteristic of female crowd activity that those with very young children do not put themselves at risk.

The October Days had profound consequences far outstripping the obvious one of bringing the king to the capital. For the women involved it was a notable consciousness-raising exercise – *we did this*. For the politicians the event, following the storming of the Bastille, aroused real fear. The pre-emptive action of the crowd, many of whom might be categorized as passive citizens[20] and those who fell even below that category, since no one ever contemplated giving them a political voice, had created fundamental change. Some welcomed the result but were appalled by the means. Some took comfort by insisting that revolutionary activity had been temporarily justifiable but now had ceased to be so since virtuous government was firmly established in the capital. Everyone agreed that its recurrence must at all costs be avoided. The enactment of a riot act in mid-October demonstrated that the élites were taking a much harsher political line on the question of popular disturbances designed to promote change. The relationship between the people of Paris and the politicians, perhaps the most sensitive of all relationships in the context of the Revolution, entered a new phase.

1790–OCTOBER 1793: THE GROWTH OF MILITANCY

The October Days inextricably linked the women of Paris to the forward movement of the Revolution. The years 1790–2 brought a growing belief amongst the *menu peuple* in themselves as the repository of revolutionary truth and as architects of a revolution which, because it existed with their connivance, must be made to incarnate their interests. The foundation of these beliefs was laid in July to October 1789.

The legislative work of the Constituent Assembly from the Riot Act to the Loi Chapelier, which restricted the right of associations to demand higher wages, the measures creating active and passive citizens, and the drawing of voting barriers within Paris which reduced the representation to the working class quartiers, were measures whose implications were not lost and which were rapidly interpreted as demonstrating a lack of commitment to popular interests. The grain supply improved in 1790–1 but the stolid refusal of peasant producers to accept revolutionary paper currency created an inflationary situation in which wages lagged behind prices. Public opinion was shaped by politicians, a developing press, public orators, and the actual experience of the market-place. By 1792 a revolutionary mentality could be discerned amongst the Paris populace, first depicted with Brueghelian vigour by Richard Cobb some thirty years ago. He drew on the rhetoric of the clubs, the sections, and the gutter press to define the assumptions of a couple, the good *sans-culotte* and his wife. Cobb was not so interested in the wife in this caricature but she exists in the same documents, albeit as the product of masculine reportage.[21]

The good *sans-culotte* and his wife were people who worked for a living and hence were price sensitive but content with honest sufficiency, a full bread bin and modest attire. They believed that the Revolution was their creation and that they must be alert to popular grievances, high prices and government corruption. They dreamed of a Utopia in which *les bienfaits de la Révolution* (which must be freedom from tyranny and deprivation) would ultimately convert all France into a paradise where the interests of the people and a recognition of its essential goodness would be the guiding principles.[22] Both believed in their own intrinsic goodness but also in the corruption of the king and his wife, his relatives, the clergy, and the nobility who in hankering after the old order jeopardized the full implementation of *les bienfaits de la Révolution*. They witnessed the flight to Varennes in June 1791 and learned of the king's invectives against the violence of the Paris masses during the October Days which were made clearly and explicitly in the letter Louis XVI left behind. They turned out to the Champ de Mars demonstration to express their hostility to Louis XVI and the new constitution in which, in their view, he had too much power and those who were passive citizens could do nothing to curtail it. This day turned very sour and indeed was a watershed in the response of authority to the assembled crowd. In part this was because of a bungle on Lafayette's part and confirmed his bad reputation with the crowd. He declared martial law against the petitioners of the Champ de Mars after hearing that the crowd had murdered two men who had crawled under the autel de la patrie to gape at women's legs and in spite of reassurances from the municipality's commissioners that the demonstration was peaceful and largely unarmed. However, neither Lafayette nor Bailly deployed the red flag to demonstrate to the crowd that it must disperse. Instead a shot was fired from within the crowd and the National Guard panicked and charged the petitioners causing considerable loss of life and infliction of wounds on the largely unarmed populace. At this point a deep bitterness emerged between the Guard and the people. A number of radical leaders were arrested, and the right of collective petitioning, which the Constituant had tried to stop, was outlawed by the Legislative Assembly.

From the very outset, the Legislative Assembly was threatened by popular disturbances. The harvest of 1791 was mediocre. As early as September 1791 there were attempts to impose *taxation populaire* in the Paris provisioning zone and January/February saw a new outcrop of grocery riots in the capital by groups of women. Initially the war seemed right to the Paris populace because they believed that foreign powers were seeking to undermine their revolution. They sent their sons to the front and made real monetary sacrifices. They responded angrily to news of military disaster, traitorous generals, and the approach of the Prussians towards Paris. They became afraid and felt betrayed by the politicians. Defeat had to be someone's fault. They looked for scapegoats. They believed themselves to be the victims of conspiracy and betrayed by their leaders. The war altered yet again the relationship of people with authority when authority was clearly not to be trusted either with the Revolution or with the people's lives.

Clearly, many aspects of what Cobb defined as the revolutionary mentality were common to both men and women. In the pages of Hébert's *Père Duchêne*, perhaps the most significant gutter press publication of the Revolution, we are, however, given some graphic details of the particular attributes of the *sans-culotte*'s wife. Honest, chaste, a good plain cook with an ugly face, clean but with a hatred of finery, mother to two or three children, one at the front, one currently being reared by her in sound revolutionary principles, a woman whose happiness was totally bound up with the well-being of her family and who was capable of brutality in its defence. She was fully prepared to confront the internal enemy at home. But what was her view of citizenship? Did she have political aspirations on her own behalf?

The evidence would suggest that her political ambitions were ambiguous and may have varied enormously. There is no evidence to suggest that the overwhelming majority of women had any political pretensions on their own behalf on the issue of the vote. However, their endorsement of the representation of the household through the husband in local and national politics appears to have been total and strong. Their own right to petition, denounce, fill the tribunes of the Assembly and later the Comités, and criticize politicians and address them as 'tu' to remind them of whose interests they were supposed to represent (emphatically, these women had no respect for a higher authority) was also strongly pressed. Spy, denouncer, critic, judge, and intense believer in the intrinsic rectitude of her assumption of these roles – *voilà la femme du sans-culotte*. Feminine *sans-culotterie* embodied a notion of citizenship for women which was not passive and which called upon them to be vigilant in the elimination of the internal enemy whilst their sons fought at the front. They were part of 'the people.' The people were strong and could, when massed, force statesmen into adopting measures designed to promote their well-being.

More than anything else, the relationship between the women of the revolutionary crowds and those of

the women's clubs reveals what the former understood
by citizenship.

The issue of women's equality with men and its promotion by women can perhaps only be allotted a small
space in the big history of the Revolution (if a large
one in the history of feminism). This is in no way to
minimize the writings and claims of individuals such
as Olympe de Gouges and Théroigne de Méricourt who
used the arguments of equality embodied in enlightenment discourse to promote the right of full citizenship for some women.[23] The claims for women's
political equality find only a faint expression in pre-
revolutionary political writing. Some argue that the ancien régime salons were a breeding ground for a greater
political awareness on the part of the women who ran
them and that there was some kind of linear development from these salons to the clubs. This is not obvious from the evidence. When club life developed
apace in 1790–2 some women, and one can name only
a handful, used the clubs to advance claims for the
natural right of women to civic parity. Olympe de
Gouges and Etta Palm d'Elders belong here. Another
early militant was Pauline Léon who on the outbreak
of war presented to the Legislative Assembly a petition
(which was denied) signed by three hundred and nine-
teen women asking to be allowed to form a *garde nationale* to defend Paris. The intention, the petition
stressed, was defensive. Women did not, when the enemy reached Paris, want to stand by and have their
throats slit like sheep. The grounds for refusing the
petition were that the order of nature would be in-
verted. Twenty days later, Théroigne de Méricourt called
for the creation of legions of amazons to defend the

Revolution and insisted that the right to bear arms turned women into citizens.[24] Pétion as mayor of the commune made some conciliatory noises suggesting that he took such initiatives seriously. To prove it he sanctioned a ceremony to honour Reine Audu, the most intrepid heroine of the October Days, with a sword 'as an authentic testimony to her bravery and patriotism.'[25] However, this may have been no more than a sop to keep the militant feminists on his side.

It is clear that the impact of these clubs remained limited. Attendance rates were very low and the declamations of de Méricourt and de Gouges appear to have fallen on stony ground. Why was this so? Perhaps the answer lies in the failure of these clubs to address issues in ways understandable to the majority of Parisian women. The clubs were sensitive to the problem of poverty, but they never talked about the price of bread, only about the obligation of women who could afford it to concern themselves with philanthropy. It is not clear that women generally wanted to fight for their country or that the political pretentions of the clubs seemed relevant to the female *sans-culotte* population. The most vociferous champions of women's natural rights tried to exert pressure on the Girondin politicians to acknowledge women's rights. Amongst the *sans-culottes* population, however, there was little sympathy for the Girondins who were elected according to a property qualification and were overtly antipathetic to any idea of popular sovereignty. Such political change might give Paris a greater amount of leverage in politics than it already had. Popular sovereignty was at the heart of the *sans-culotte* agenda. The Girondins also exercised political authority under a constitution which in the eyes of the Jacobins and the *sans-culottes* gave too much power to the monarch, who was seen as a traitor. After April 1792, the Girondins were also encumbered with a war, undertaken to advance their political strength and rally a dissident nation, which turned to immediate disaster. Within months, the enemy were within miles of Paris. This military involvement caused an overnight devaluation of the assignat with significant consequences for the wage earner. Moreover, the Girondins were explicitly committed to laissez-faire in the grain trade. Though in fact in the context of the Revolution this did not necessarily mean that they would abandon subsidies for bread on the Paris market, laissez-faire was associated with the freedom of the market-place and the removal of restrictions on the movement of grain, which in turn were associated with problems of shortages. In brief, any perceived linkage between the women of the clubs and the Girondin faction ensured the hostility of Parisian working women.

However, Le Club des citoyennes républicaines révolutionnaires, founded in May 1793 with the express purpose of combating hoarding and inflation – critical issues for the *sans-culottes* – had a quite different relevance. This club is of real interest to the historian of the Revolution because it profoundly worried the Comité de salut public.[26] It raised the spectre of intervention in politics by women on the scale of the October Days. The Jacobin leadership and the police feared an alliance might develop with the leaders of the women's club serving as bridge, between the women of the Paris working *quartiers* and the *enragés*, militants who stood for a much stricter policing of the sale of grain, a more intense war against hoarders and speculators, an acceleration of the Terror, and a reapplication of the Constitution of 1793, put into limbo by the Convention while France was at war. If that alliance had come into full effect, it could be argued that the Revolution would have moved, however temporarily, more emphatically to the left. Certainly, this club threatened to build a bridge between the women of the organized club and working-class women by giving female citizenship a positive role, placing the war on hoarders and the crusade against the internal enemy in their hands. Unlike earlier clubs, this one was prepared to use the masses to achieve its end. It put the club leaders in competition with the Jacobin politicians for control over the engendered crowd. In one sense two traditions met, the relatively new one of structured political organization through a women's club and the age-old one of direct female action which had produced the October Days. However, this alliance, in so far as it had real form, should not disguise the divisions between the women's clubs interpreted as Girondin or royalist or, indeed, some divisions between the Club des citoyennes républicaines révolutionnaires and those women of the quartiers who undertook piecemeal protests in bread queues. The leaders of the Club des citoyennes républicaines révolutionnaires believed in organized and concerted action to achieve their political and economic ends and interpreted random action as wasted energy.

Let us consider the evolution of the alliance between the new club and the old tradition in the context of the events of 1793. In the early days of the Convention (February 1793) a series of grocery riots in which women were to the fore were mounted over the rising cost of bread and, more fundamentally, interruptions in supplies or total shortages in critical areas.[27] A substantial

delegation of women went to the Convention and denounced free trade – defended by politicians of all hues
– as licence for the oppression of the poor. In mid-
February, a delegation of washerwomen demanded the
death penalty for hoarders of soap, a commodity that
was essential to their livelihood. The leader of the *enragés*, Jacques Roux, encouraged, even if he did not
orchestrate, a series of riots on 25–26 February. This
time the women simply pillaged the stalls and shops
where the basic commodity prices were beyond their
reach. Soap, sugar, and candles were distributed at what
was deemed a fair price. If washerwomen were hard
hit by the price of soap, the cost of candles was particularly worrying for those who needed to work after
dark during the winter months. The National Guard
moved in to help the stall holders and disperse the
women but Chaumette, the procurator of the commune, informed the Comité de salut public that without a harsher law against hoarding there was no chance
of order among the women on a permanent basis.[28]
Roux himself had an enormous appeal to women as
the red priest of the *bon sans-culotte Jésus Christ*. He
concentrated on measures against speculation and vi-
tuperative attacks on the Girondins and their friends
in the ministry, who stood between the people and *les
bienfaits de la Révolution*. Further troubles were expected. Indeed demonstrations were celebrated in advance and did not necessarily live up to their promised
strength. However, public order was obviously maintained with difficulty. This was perhaps not surprising.
Voyer d'Argenson noted in his journal for this month
that 'more than eight hundred persons have perished
from destitution in the Faubourg Saint Antoine between 20 January and 20 February, that these poor

people die of cold and hunger in their garrets, that the priests arrive too late, to see them die without being able to help.'[29]

From February and to try to calm the situation, the price of bread in Paris was fixed at three sous the pound, a low price. The problem then became, and remained so throughout the year, largely a question of short supply. The Jacobin municipality sought to ensure fairness by posting two police *commissaires* outside the bakers' shops to see that opening hours were respected and hence that there was no apparent selling under the counter and also that the contentious queues were kept under some control. These efforts did not stop a deputation of women from the Faubourg Saint Antoine on 1 May 1793 to demand energetic measures to reform the army and to impose a maximum price for bread. The Convention was occupied and, although the deputies voted to suspend the session, the women threatened that their occupation would not cease until their demands were realized. The result was that on 4 May a departmental maximum on grain and flour was decreed.

Ten days later, the Club des citoyennes républicaines révolutionnaires was formed. The deliberations of this club remain something of a mystery. We know nothing of the size of its membership. One estimate is as low as sixty-seven, another one hundred. Dominique Godineau thinks that one hundred and seventy attended the initial meeting. The women claimed the support of thousands and the Jacobins certainly believed that their program could rally women on a massive scale. The records of its deliberations have been lost or deliberately destroyed by the police or taken by the members of the club after its closure to destroy the evidence that

could be used against former members. In the climate
of the day this made sense. The club seems from the
signatures to petitions to have largely been composed
of small tradeswomen who could at least sign their
names. The leaders were militants prepared to use the
right of petitioning, to organize mass demonstrations,
and to make a nuisance of themselves to further their
ends. These women were – and Marat amongst others
extolled their single-mindedness – calling for a war on
hoarders and a plentiful supply of bread and the overthrow of the Girondin faction. They believed that concerted and planned action was the best way to achieve
success.

The club's commitment to overthrow the Girondins
certainly coincided with a vital Jacobin priority. The
Jacobins in 1793 were locked in a hostile factional contest to eliminate their Girondin rivals. Any help that
could be given in this direction was more than wel-
come. The energy of the club activists was striking:
endorsing petitions from the Cordeliers for an acceleration of the Terror and insisting that the Girondins
be publicly tried for treason and misconduct of the war;
systematically attempting to enter the Convention
without tickets to harass and heckle the Girondin deputies, and preventing their supporters from entering the
tribunes. These supporters included the intrepid, if
highly individualistic promoter of women's citizenship,
(narrowly defined for she was no friend of the masses)
Théroigne de Méricourt. On 15 May a group of *femmes
patriotes* set upon her as she was about to enter the
tribunes. The ensuing flagellation was exceedingly violent and the would-be *amazone* was rescued from an
even worse fate, it is alleged, by Marat. This event had
been threatened for a few weeks and a plate adorned

with a token set of buttocks promptly appeared for sale. Indeed, it seems to have been a characteristic of women's activities within the Revolution to secure maximum attention by advance warning. The flagellation of de Méricourt, who was known to be a monarchist and a Girondin supporter, symbolizes the split between the women outside the Convention and the early *clubistes*.[30] However, the act was intended as just one in a series designed to undermine the Girondin politicians. In the memoires of these deputies, the women who filled the tribunes come in for the utmost opprobrium. Gorsas says that the women alone prevented them speaking and swaying the Convention and denied them the means to defend themselves. Isnard addressed the Convention on 25 May 1793, and warned of an impending massacre of the Right in these terms: 'The pretext will be a manufactured outbreak of disorder in the Convention; the women will set things going: indeed a regiment of them has already been formed for this iniquitous work.'[31] On 28 May, Lecointre reported an appeal to the Jacobins by the women's club to lead an insurrection.[32]

In the tense weeks of Jacobin-Girondin conflict preceding the Paris uprising of 31 May these women played an important role in determining that the people of the streets were solidly anti-Girondin. One police agent reported that 'evil influences, under the mark of patriotism, have excited these revolutionary heroines to riot and to take up arms so as to dissolve the Convention and cause rivers of blood to flow in Paris.'[33] In the events of 31 May to 2 June which reached a climax in the surrounding of the Assembly by a combined force of National Guards and *sans-culottes* aimed at the arrest of the Girondin deputies, we hear from Gorsas that those who attempted flight were stopped by *une troupe de femmes se disant révolutionnaires, troupe de furies, avide de carnage.*[34] How many of the women activists of those days actually belonged to the club it is impossible to say. However, *sans-culotte* women could justifiably feel they had played a positive role in the fall of the Girondins.

Yet after the end of June, now unimpeded by their political rivals, the Jacobins did not need such support. Furthermore, the militant leaders had opposed the Girondins without necessarily committing themselves to any other politician. Indeed, they accused the Jacobin representatives of procrastinating over the introduction of more stringent measures against hoarders and speculators. In the last week of June, economic skirmishes over the price of needful commodities resumed. Police reports dwelt on incidents provoked by shortages of loaves in bread queues.

The murder of Marat in his bath on 13 July occasioned an intensification of the belief that good patriots were surrounded by enemies. The club and groups of militant women seized a special role in the funeral cortège carrying the bath in which Marat's bloody body continued to exude blood and subsequently they paraded with the blood-stained shirt and empty bath through the streets.[35] The event led to demands for an intensification of the Terror. By the end of August, it was possible to discern a breach between Lacombe and the dominant Robespierrist party in which she charged the politicians with deliberately delaying the arrest of suspects and demanded an intensification of the Terror.[36] Pauline Léon simultaneously proposed in the club that it should press for new elections and a prompt introduction of the Jacobin constitution (voted in June

1793 but immediately put on ice) because too many politicians had become idle and *ils traînent sur les bancs* – a favourite concept justifying pre-emptive action by women.[37]

This was talk which signified the abrupt termination of any honeymoon period between the *clubistes* and the Jacobin politicians. Lacombe and Léon were also progressively suspected of a liaison with the *enragé* leaders. It is from this point that the relationship between the *clubistes* and the *enragés* becomes increasingly difficult to fathom. Certainly the female militants were not a subcategory of the *enragés* and up to the end of June the Républicaines had been critical of Roux and his methods. In the summer, however, Léon became the mistress of Leclerc, an *enragé* leader, and one who certainly believed militant women essential if the *enragé* agenda was to be realized. Personal linkages made it possible for their enemies to see the *clubistes* as the handmaidens of Roux and his followers and this association was to prove in the end disastrous.[38]

A schism between the dominant Robespierrist group in the Convention and Roux surfaced in late June with the *enragé* leader's famous manifesto on the obligations of government to a hungry populace, a document, incidentally, which is one of the few to mention the particular plight of the woman dependent upon the work of her hands.[39] Roux's solution to France's problems was admittedly crude. He wanted a new 'September massacre' of hoarders and speculators and government action to force shopkeepers to carry on their trade without personal profit (and we should not forget this aspect of the *enragé* platform).[40] Robespierre embarked upon the systematic destruction of the individual he saw as a threat to the maintenance of order. Roux was arrested first in August, released, and then rearrested on 5 September.

The need to retain control of Paris and maintain order in the capital was fully apparent to the Robespierrist politicians. On 4 September there was a huge demonstration with a mass petition. Jacobin activists were responsible for the event, and won the tardy approval of the commune. They invited sectional delegations, to present themselves, without arms but with banners, demanding purges of aristocrats and the formation of an *armée révolutionnaire*. It converged on the Convention and that body agreed to put Terror on the order of the day and to the formation of an *armée révolutionnaire*.[41] It was an orchestrated, controlled demonstration, though one which served to alarm by its intensity the more moderate Jacobins. The Robespierrists knew that something had to be delivered which would satisfy the city masses and that Paris's tranquillity could only be purchased through concessions, however troubling they might be. A day later, Barère denounced the counter-revolutionaries who were stirring up the women over the subsistence question. The same night Roux was rearrested. Amongst his papers was found a letter which referred plainly to his desire to mobilize the women of Paris if the *enragé* agenda to carry the Revolution further to the left was to be achieved. 'Victory is certain as soon as the women mix with the *sans-culottes*. They have the doubly advantageous attribute of conquering men through charm and through fearlessness. We are approaching the moment when we can rouse a considerable mass of republicans to crush tyranny.'[42]

The arrest of Roux was followed by that of Varlet on 18 September. The latter had spoken out to resist the attempts made in the decree of 9 September to strip the section revolutionary committees of their right to arrest public functionaries. The Club des citoyennes républicaines révolutionnaires could not remain silent. A police agent, Soulet, reported hearing Lacombe in the club denounce the Convention's police committee, the Committee of General Security, for arresting the best patriots.[43] This report was to give Chabot and Basire the chance to formulate an elaborate and damaging story that Lacombe lobbied the committee for the release of counter-revolutionaries.

Deputations and petitions to the Convention allegedly claiming to represent 4675 citizenesses demanded the arrest of more nobles and suspects and an accelerated clearance of the guilty in the prisons. Lacombe was skating on thin ice. On 16 September the Jacobin club did order her arrest and her rooms were searched but nothing found and so no further action was taken.[44]

The link between the militants of the Club des citoyennes républicaines révolutionnaires and the *enragés* was never fully explicit. If Lacombe had been, and Léon was, the mistress of Leclerc, a close relationship with the *enragés* was not acceptable to all members of the club. The support of the *enragés*, as Rose has shown, was largely drawn from the least economically privileged of Parisian society and was arguably more marginal and certainly more anarchic than that of all but the most militant of the *sans-culottes*. Roux's committment to ensuring that his poorest parishioners were fed was wholehearted and total. His compassion for those with empty stomachs knew no bounds and his critical biographers and commentators never call his sincerity into account. Varlet and Leclerc came from more substantial families and each had a small private income. They carried with them the reputation of being hotheads.[45] The president of the Club des citoyennes républicaines révolutionnaires was uncomfortable about any alliance with this group and resigned over the issue, whereupon control fell to Lacombe and Léon. It was a transfer of power that did not pass unnoticed. The ability of women to disrupt the course of politics was not lost on the politicians of the sections and of the commune, and the political clubs and their potential to do so disquieted them. Chabot on 16 September 1793 in the Jacobins grumbled: 'It is these counter-revolutionary *bougresses* [sluts] who cause all the riotous outbreaks, above all over bread. They made a revolution over coffee and sugar, and they will make others if we don't watch out.'[46]

The arrest of Roux was the first instalment of what emerged as Jacobin crowd policy. This could be summarized as follows: first, strip the crowd of its leadership and hence its capacity to compel change; second, atomize the crowd if possible, sever its elements the one from the other; third, orchestrate the crowd, organize its demonstrations and direct them to specific ends or endow them with a harmless purpose like the fête or with an acceptably focused hatred like the assistance at the guillotine; finally, cede and exceed on the demands concerning bread. If the *sans-culottes* population wanted death to hoarders, it could take comfort in the government's new measures to extend the maximum.

Each element of this four-point strategy involved a matter concerning women. After the arrests of Roux and Varlet came the closure of the Société républicaine révolutionnaire on 30 September in order to put an end to the militant activities of its leaders and destroy their potential for raising a broader following. This was an example of atomization.

The agents of the closure were the Dames de la Halle – the market women who had been prominent on 5 October. These women had been positively alienated from the *enragés* and the women's clubs which they saw as a direct threat to their livelihood. Their trade had been severely dislocated in the course of 1792–3 by grain shortages whether the result of peasant withholding or the other meteorological reasons given for the inadequacy of grain deliveries. They considered themselves the victims of city or section administrators, who, in the name of waging war against speculators and the black market, found it easier to attack the petty stall operators than the big grain merchants. They were deeply resentful of the indiscriminate pillaging and intimidation of Roux and his followers. The location of the women's club in Saint Eustache added insult to injury and made the market women ever more vulnerable to what they discerned as prying in their business and possible denunciation for malpractice. From the *enragés* they anticipated piecemeal attack.

The ground for conflict between the market women and the Club des citoyennes républicaines révolutionnaires, however, was ostensibly the compulsion on women to wear the *sans-culotte* emblem, the revolutionary cockade which had been made obligatory for all citizens. The women of the clubs espoused this cause. The *marchandes* argued that the cockade implied full citizenship which carried with it the obligation to bear arms and to fight. This, they claimed, was contrary to their rights as women. Initially the municipality was not sympathetic to the *marchandes* but suddenly (and one would like to know on whose instructions) it changed its tack and insisted that women who were not destined to concern themselves with politics were free to chose whether or not to bedeck themselves with the symbols of citizenship. The *marchandes* on 28 October savagely broke up a meeting of the club and a day later petitioned not merely to be released from the obligation of wearing the cockade but for the closure of the women's club. This was an interesting coupling of issues. They won on both counts. It is, as Barry Rose, historian of the *enragés*, pointed out, difficult to resist the conclusion that the *marchandes* were encouraged by Robespierrist elements anxious to carry further the liquidation of the *enragé* opposition.[47] Or, the weakening of organized women's resistance was too good an opportunity to miss. The exploitation of an apparent split in the ranks of working women was to these politicians a gift. It made possible the isolation and marginalization of activists in the Républicaines révolutionnaires. The desire to get the female crowd back into the home, to deny it citizenship, and to exclude it from sectional and other meetings was expressed in a flurry of rhetoric from Amar in the Convention, who insisted that 'a woman's honour confined her to the private sphere and precluded her from a struggle with men.'[48] Waiting in the wings was Sophie who was trotted out as a model for the discourse.

Whatever the link between some of the *clubistes* and the *enragés* and the desire to stem the voice of criticism emanating from an institution run by women, many of the recent histories of women during the Revolution seize upon latent Jacobin antifeminism as the overriding reasons for the closure of the club. Certainly that antifeminism was there; but the timing of the closure within the context of a concerted attack upon the *en-*

ragés and the use of market women who had been the targets of Roux's inflammatory exhortations to pillage strongly suggest that more practical considerations were at issue. The Paris commune itself, with Chaumette as its procurator, was struggling to keep the market adequately provisioned, and deeply critical of the Républicaines révolutionnaires. The scanty evidence that we have also suggests that the club was divided amongst itself. The Commune closed the club hoping to reduce the evident tension and perceived threat to public order generated by market disturbances at the first opportunity. Thereafter, it dealt with individual, discontented and frustrated female purchasers in the bread queues.

Some aspects of Jacobin crowd manipulation were designed to appease women. Consider woman's role as mother heroine figure in the Republican fête as orchestrated in Paris. Here she is exalted as nurturer and for her readiness to sacrifice. She is drawn into the celebrations and made a significant force critical to state and society. In a different vein, the *tricoteuse* knitting for the war effort in front of the guillotine as the internal conspiracy is annihilated before her eyes expressed yet another form of patriotic, canalized emotion which confirmed and did not threaten the political status quo – unless, of course, she demanded more blood than the government was prepared to spill.

Two points stand out. First, there was no widespread protest at the disbanding of the Républicaines révolutionnaires or expressed protest at the elimination of women from a separate club life, which in any case had never attracted women on a large scale. Second, the maximum and the policing which enforced it were deeply appreciated by the female consumer. From October 1793, organized and separate political organization for women disappeared, although a few scores of women continued to attend clubs admitting both sexes. However, on the streets and in the market, a new breed of female militancy surfaced as working women, *sans-culotte* wives above all, familiarized themselves with a body of law that was, they believed, designed to protect their interests as consumers and whose enforcement was backed by the guillotine.

Suzanne Peterson has demonstrated how a cognizance of the terms of the regulations promptly became part of the buyer's savoir faire. Traditional notions of a moral economy blended with democratic principle to produce vigilant market practice. Perrière, an observer of the Paris scene in the late autumn, marvelled at a woman who brought a butcher flouting the regulations to account. She took the goods, calculated their value by reference to the maximum, and when asked for more, smartly tendered no more than the law demanded. She told the butcher that the price might not suit him but *c'est celui de la loi*.[49]

BREAD AND THE CONSTITUTION OF 1793: OCTOBER 1793 TO SPRING 1795

The maximum put the *femme du sans-culotte* on side of the Jacobin dictatorship. The efforts made by the Comité de Salut Public for the provisioning of the capital inspired some, if not total, confidence that government was committed to the interests of the *menu peuple*. This did not mean that grumbling ceased. Throughout the winter of 1793–4 everyone in Paris had complaints to make about the quality and supply of foodstuffs but on the whole, the maximum worked for them. The government was conscious that a hungry capital spelled political instability and was prepared to put the full force of the Terror behind its provisioning policy. Paris was given priority over everywhere else. The feeding of the capital and that of the army were placed on the same footing; much of provincial France was stripped of food and subjected to the unambiguous thuggery of the *armées révolutionnaires* in order to keep food pouring into the capital.[50]

The effort needed to sustain the grain flow to the capital in face of a peasantry deeply resentful of price fixation strained every level of government. In the winter of 1794 a certain political apathy seems to have settled on the capital. Attendance at the clubs even by the male *sans-culotte* declined sharply. Political purges passed without popular response. Were the people lulled into false somnolence by the apparent victory of the controlled economy and the improvement in France's military performance? Even the fall of Robespierre in July 1794 did not trouble the surface of Parisian political life. Stripped of their leaders by the purges, the populace watched in confusion as one group of terrorist politicians ousted another and popular leaders were one by one eliminated. Roux, Varlet, Vincent, Hebert, Danton, and finally Robespierre had all claimed to represent their interests and in turn had been removed from the political spectrum. Of what significance could Robespierre's downfall be to them?

The harvest reaped in the late summer of 1794 was one of the worst northern Europe had ever experienced. The controlled economy which had largely operated to the advantage of Paris had not been able to prevent severe problems even as early as spring 1794 in many provincial towns and villages in spite of the efforts of local administrators.[51] In many small towns, particularly in the Paris provisioning zone which extended for about a hundred miles around the city, riots began as early as April over shortages which were linked to peasant counter-revolutionary activity. The dearth was declared 'artificial' because, it was officially held, the harvest of 1793 had been good.

The same story and deflection of urban hatred away from the government to the peasantry and counter-revolutionary forces could not be told after the harvest of 1794. The problem of keeping Paris supplied rapidly intensified.

The thermidoreans, those politicians who manoeuvred the fall of Robespierre and his closest colleagues, were unwilling to put the mechanism of the Terror behind the enforcement of a controlled economy and insisted that the shortages were the result of terrorist thuggery which had alienated the peasant producer and that only the return to a free market economy would save the day. Of all the U-turns made by this new group of politicians, this was the one that was to sound the most dissonant chord in the ears of the Paris populace. By December 1794, in an attempt to get grain flowing, the government abandoned the maximum and printed more paper money to cope with its war purchasing – to some extent on foreign markets. It recognized the need to maintain bread subsidies in the capital. However, it allowed a free market to exist as well for those who could afford it. All commodities except grain and meat (whose price was raised from fourteen to twenty-one sous per pound) were free to find their 'natural' level. Coal, candles, soap, and groceries disappeared from the market stalls as producers refused to deal in goods in exchange for a debased currency. Inflation embarked upon a rapid upward spiral and prices escalated.

The winter of 1794–5 was murderous. The Seine froze. It was bitterly cold. Although bread was subsidized and rationed, the supply was irregular and inadequate. By February, Parisians collapsed in the streets from inanition produced by a bread ration which on many days barely touched ten ounces and on some days fell to two. Those who could afford it purchased in the 'free' market. The existence of this market exacerbated popular perceptions of the plight of the poor. It was evident that the rich ate whilst nursing mothers lost their milk and watched their babies die sucking at empty breasts. Amenorrhoea set in. The bread queues formed overnight and in these queues, largely of women, the complaints were vociferous: complaints of betrayal by politicians, of the waste of their lives and their loved ones in the service of a revolution which had turned its back on the people who had striven to promote it. There was a sense of bitterness, a feeling of waste. Some fantasized about the ancien régime and harked back to *un bon vieux temps* which had never existed. Some saw divine retribution for the destruction of the Catholic religion. Some blamed the politicians and added threats: 'il viendra un temps ou l'on marquera les députés sur le front avec un fer rouge ... on ira à la Convention leur mettre le pistolet sur la gorge et les renvoyer.'[52]

These threats were reported in police files. However, there was no vision of an alternative to the Convention but rather a re-emergence of a demand for new elections which would end the provisional government and re-establish the people's deputies.

One can multiply instances of the rhetoric involved in these demands. Some called for a return to the days of Robespierre and the rivers of blood which had forced *l'aristocratie meurtrière du cultivateur* to hand over its grain. There were daily instances of protest and pillaging by women outside the bakers. Germinal (27 March) saw the beginning of women's protests to the Convention (some totalling several hundreds). Usually twenty were let in. The Convention, conscious of the build-up to revolt, began to move troops into the city. As the bread ration plummeted to as low as four ounces per day the final *journées* of the popular revolution – the events of germinal and prairial – were prepared.

If 12 germinal was an affair for both men and women in the final demonstration to the Convention, its inception was female orchestrated. We hear again a familiar vocabulary in police reports coming from the mouths of women ... les hommes traînent ... les hommes sont des lâches; my good for nothing husband is standing by and letting his family starve ... what sort of a man watches his wife and children die from hunger?[53] It was also in part a replication of 4 September 1793 which had worked so well: a mass demonstration of unarmed men from each of the working-class sections with banners and petitions and the strong and simple slogan *du pain et la constitution.*

The people went into the Convention unarmed. They shouted. They did not heed the supplications of the remaining Jacobin deputies to go home. They were promised bread. They went outside. They pillaged. They fell into fights with *muscadins*, the name given to organized gangs recruited from middle-class youths and army deserters who proclaimed themselves as 'antiterrorist' but engaged in thuggery themselves, and

members of the National Guard who remained loyal
to the government. There may at the beginning of the
day have been as many as ten thousand men and
women involved but they fell away and the women in
particular went home.

The incident was used by the thermidoreans to purge
the Convention of its remaining Jacobins and the rump,
try as it might, had no means to increase the flow of
bread to Paris. Within weeks, another rising had occurred, that of 1 prairial (20 May). This *journée* was in
essence a last-ditch plea, a woman's event terrible in
its poignancy. Perhaps the men had lost heart after the
failure of germinal. Without alternatives, the women
made a massive round-up of their neighbours and
women in the popular *quartiers*, in the streets, on the
staircases. The last occupation of the Convention was
almost entirely by women.

They went for the final protest in the context of the
Revolution to the seat of power unarmed. A certain
citoyen Canton, *coiffeur*, who turned up to help with
weapons was sent home by *une vendeuse de salades*
with the following words: 'ceux qui prendraient les
armes étaient des couillons.'[54]

The National Guard tried to drive them from the
tribunes with whips. But whips did not work and they
used the butt ends of bayonets instead. Blood was spilt.
The rumour – they are killing our women – got out
into the crowd outside and the seething crowd tried to
come to their defence. But there were armed forces to
hold the crowd and this was the prelude to the three
or four days of fighting that resulted in the disarming
of the *faubourgs*. The Faubourg Saint Antoine was invested with a battalion of almost twenty thousand
troops and surrendered without a shot although the

women tried to resist the handing over of the cannon. It was the last vestige of their strength. They had taken a cannon to Versailles in October 1789 but at that stage the women and the National Guard were on the same side.

The rising failed because the Convention could not deliver the goods. It could not get more bread for the people. It also failed because no body of politicians was prepared to take the side of the people in order to forward their own careers and because the people themselves did not want to destroy the Convention before new elections had been decreed. The rising was not merely about bread, though it might not have occurred without economic hardship, but had distinct political demands which included the release of patriot prisoners, a freely elected Paris commune, and, of course, new elections. The restoration of popular sovereignty was the only guarantee that the interests of the people, as interpreted by the people of Paris, would be respected. Those who participated in the rising were not so naïve as to imagine that bread would be delivered without government. The riot, however, had nowhere to go unless new elections were conceded. The days of the revolutionary crowd existing to carry the Revolution forward into a new and more radical phase were over. The defeat was an important turning point marking the end of the 'popular' phase of the Revolution.

The gendered crowd of the Revolution links the riots of traditional France with unfolding revolutionary politics. It demonstrates the dynamic of crowd formation and reveals a sense of legitimation as the mouthpiece of the innocent. In the last riots of the Revolution the role of women as inciters but also as perpetrators of a particular kind of mass demonstration stands out. The women go right to the top, as in October 1789. They confront authority largely unarmed (certainly without firearms) as the innocent empowered to speak on the part of their suffering families. Their message to authority is that they come in peace but that if they fail more drastic measures must be taken. They are intrepid at the outset but they melt away once the weaponry gains in sophistication and the real fighting begins. They do not expect (meaning traditionally find right) that women will be fired on, and the increasing propensity of authority to do this – and the Revolution constitutes a watershed here – is perhaps what ultimately drives women from the nineteenth-century crowd. The *prairial* crowd had, however, a political sophistication which it had learned over the preceding two years. A pamphlet, *Insurrection du peuple pour obtenir du pain et reconquérir ses droits*, was distributed by women to the insurgents during the days before the disturbance. The tactic of entering the tribunes and preventing the politicians from making themselves heard as they had done during the Girondin crisis was tried again by the women. The *prairial* crowd was arguably the most violent of all the women's *journées* in the Revolution and one deputy, Féraud, may have met his death at their hands.[55]

The *prairial* crowd was not optimistic and it did not perceive any alternative to its strategy. We do not know the size of the initial crowd of women.[56] One report says two thousand, and if this is so, then it is clear that many had lost hope or had pinned their hopes elsewhere and had abandoned popular demonstration, regarding it as unlikely to solve their predicament. We are on the eve of a great popular religious revival in the capital and it was arguably one born of despair.

Indeed, it is to be compared with the aftermath of the Commune in 1871. The police noted two queues which it considered equally to be feared, *une à la messe l'autre à la boulangerie*. This short-lived religious revival, made possible because the thermidoreans were initially committed to religious tolerance as a means of reconciling peasant France, fed on guilt – *culpa mea*. Women who had abandoned religious commitment in the great dechristianizing wave which had spread over the capital in 1793–4 sought out the solace of religion. The confessionals were full.[57]

The number of bodies of both sexes fished out of the Seine also hit record levels.[58] If 1789 was the year of hope, 1795 was that of despair, the one in which all hope and passion were indeed spent.

The thermidoreans did not have recourse to a policy of mass arrests and victimization of individuals in order to subdue the populace. Perhaps they did not want to create popular martyrs. Perhaps the disarming of the *faubourgs* was sufficient to reassure them that the strength of the crowd was emasculated. In spite of the order to arrest all the women who had been responsible for inciting others to revolt, only 148 names appear in the police dossiers. Of these about a quarter had a past political record as militants. Of the thirty-nine women whose ages are given, the majority were over forty-five or under thirty. Those with young children were, as usual, absent from the female crowd. All the women over fifty who involved themselves seem to have had previous records in rioting crowds. Many participants were still teenagers. Most were wage earners. Two-thirds could sign their names.[59]

Individual dossiers give telling details. A stonemason called Decloux defended his wife and teenage daughter against the charge of being 'Jacobines enragées' with the declaration that they 'n'ont été Jacobines que comme toutes les autres femmes d'ouvriers qu'on avait imprégnées d'opinions et de maximes.'[60] The allusion to the politicization of the previous years could take other forms. Some were anxious to escape a prison sentence and were prepared to repent the error of their ways. The femme Saint Prix confessed: 'Je n'ai pu me garantir de l'ascendent qu'ont exercé sur mon esprit des imposteurs dont le patriotisme apparent m'avait séduite. J'ai cru en me livrant à leurs insinuations mensongères servir ici mon pays comme mon époux et mes enfants le servaient aux armées.'[61] This was a clever defence and perhaps an astringent reminder of the plight of the woman trying to live on a military pension. There were several analogous tales. The strongest and most vociferous of militant women laid claim to the sweetness and docility of their sex rendered temporarily distraught by the effects of suffering upon their families. They insisted on their special vulnerability as women in face of the hardship of the times. Others used the ploy of being of *un certain âge* and hence endowed with the irrationality that was the particular product of the menopause. In short, to spare themselves a prison sentence, they colluded in the reconstruction of a female stereotype which for years had allowed them easy treatment before the courts. On the whole, they were successful. Forty per cent of the accused were immediately released and the overwhelming majority of the rest secured two-month prison sentences.

Perhaps of greater significance than the trials themselves was the package of laws which were enacted over the next few months with the purpose of silencing women. Within a week of the rising of prairial came prohibitions on their entering the tribunes; then a decree prohibiting them from participation in any political assembly. Next (4 prairial) came the unanimous decision that women should retire to their homes and that groups of more than five women gathering in the street were liable to arrest.[62] The wives of former Jacobin politicians were requested to return to their former departments of abode and there were cries for the judgment of the women leaders of the revolt by a military tribunal though the Convention here drew back. The entire collection of measures, however, reveals the depth of fear felt by the politicians for the women. They had proved the staunchest and most intrepid defenders of popular sovereignty, political animals who had dared to remind the government of its obligations. This package was therefore more than just gratuitous antifeminism. It was an attempt to silence once and for all the engendered crowd.

Other laws followed at a more leisurely pace. There was the attempt to curtail the number of war widows whose husbands had not been Paris residents living in the capital.[63] At all costs, the politicians wanted to remove from the streets of the capital critical women and particularly those whose plight might justifiably arouse popular sympathy. They could do less damage in a provincial town.

Silence, the politicians had learned, had to start with women. They had to be stopped from inciting riot, for without that incitement there could be no riot. If the women were prevented from gathering together they would not generate the courage to protest and individual insurgents could be dealt with by the police. If the numbers of war widows and women living on military pensions were reduced then the grievances of the wives of heroes could not be used to legitimate and hallow criticism of the government and the inadequacy of its policies. There is nothing more revelatory of government fears and guilt than these legislative initiatives and little that the collection does not tell us about the role of city women in Revolution. This body of laws constituted an inglorious end, an unworthy codicil to the history of the engendered crowd in the French Revolution. The popular revolution was indeed over and it was evident that popular sovereignty was dead beyond recall. The last to evoke it and to attempt to enforce it were two thousand grandmothers, war widows, and poor working women. We might look upon their protest as a poignant epitaph for the people's revolution.

CHAPTER TWO

Poverty and Charity: Revolutionary Mythology and Real Women

Poverty and Charity:
Revolutionary
Mythology and
Real Women

The religious institutions devoted to succouring the poor
and serving the sick are amongst those most commanding
of respect. There is perhaps nothing greater on this earth
than the sacrifice that the delicate sex makes of its beauty
and its youth in caring within hospitals for every kind of
wretched human suffering, the very sight of which is so
humiliating to mankind's pride and so offensive to our
sensibilities.

Voltaire, *Oeuvres Complètes*, 52 vols. (Paris 1877–85), xii
p344

the services that are rendered in hospitals by pure zeal
and by the sole motive of the love of God differ from and
are much more beneficial to the poor than those services
which are rendered by stewards who act most often by
no other motive than that of self-interest.

Archives Municipales, Montpellier Registre 19, July 1663

In the autumn of 1789, the National Assembly, confronted with debts whose size it could only imagine, annexed the property of the church with a view to selling it. The proceeds from the sales were to serve as backing for its paper currency, the assignat. Virtually simultaneously, it pronounced a moratorium on religious vows and proceeded to set up a standing committee, the Comité Ecclésiastique, to sort out the complexities of coping with considerable numbers of secular and regular clergy who depended on the income from land and privileges belonging to the church. The politicians were prepared to acknowledge that there would be problems. As children of the Enlightenment, a high proportion of the deputies, including some of the clerics, were convinced that church wealth, accumulated during periods of 'gothic' superstition, was an ill-gotten gain that belonged more appropriately to the nation. In the new France now being created by the Revolution, such property would be reassumed by the state and then sold to the people on terms which would have to be closely worked out. The Assembly, however, was in something of a hurry since it needed resources for the day-to-day running of the country. It announced that existing religious would have the alternatives of disbanding with a life pension or of staying together in a designated reception centre which would not necessarily respect distinctions between religious orders. However, those religious who were perceived to be carrying out important social functions, namely the running of the hospitals and institutions aimed at relieving the deserving poor, were told to remain at their posts. The Assembly believed that the way to achieve the perfect society was through the right laws.

Enlightenment rhetoric insisted upon the futility of a life dedicated to prayer to a deity whose existence could not be proved and upon the immorality of ecclesiastical wealth which had allowed a decadent minority of the population to wax fat, but it would not expose the sick to an immediate loss of nursing services and hence made them an exception to its new rules. For the rest, the message that the politicians sought to convey was that they were superfluous to the new France. Even those dedicated to social work would not in the future be joined by new recruits living under any kind of religious vow. The politicians were prepared to respect the work that the nursing sisters were doing but not their dedication to the service of God.

The Assembly was anxious to do right by as many as possible. It offered the clerics a new start. It did not know exactly what direction it envisaged for the men but an educated man with a pension to fall back on could surely find absorption into administrative activity. It believed, however, that it offered women something of inestimable worth. Without doubt it had a clear vision of the imminent happiness it intended to bestow on the ex-nun. There existed in the intellectual baggage of the Assembly a model, mythical nun. She was young, beautiful, and distressed. Her avaricious family, to save itself a dowry, had forced her into the convent. It had thus, at a blow, severed her from her natural destiny of wife and mother. Her copious breasts, symbol of natural woman, since denied her natural function must shrivel in the convent beneath her veil. As a result of revolutionary law, the nun's body would be put to its right purpose. In the convent her lot had been one of frustration since she was cut off from the realization of her true self. Perhaps she had even suffered lascivious unnatural advances from women constrained like her in this alien environment.

It will be immediately apparent to those with any familiarity with French literature that the script, as it were, for this presentation had been written by Diderot – though he drew upon a stock image. The presentation was called *La Religieuse* and the name of the nun was Suzanne. She was beautiful, fragile, abused, and in search of a man to solve her predicament. The Assembly saw itself, albeit fleetingly because it had a lot of work on its hands, as the knight on the white charger rescuing the distressed damsel of the copious bosom from a fate worse than death – namely, spinsterdom. The politicians, predictably, had views on spinsterdom. It emanated from unfair inheritance laws. It intended to standardize and allow each child, irrespective of sex and place in the family, an equal claim to the parents' property. The politicians' Suzanne would hence in the future, because none of this could be made retroactive, control as much property as did her brothers. In the interim a lump sum and a pension would facilitate her integration into society. Her ecstatic exodus would go on record as *un des bienfaits de la Révolution*. A plethora of prints even offered the exiting nun a prospective husband in the form of the ex-monk. I am not sure that this happy alternative was ever mentioned in political debates but it certainly has a strong visual presence. It would be nice to think, however, that some pungent caricaturist perceived the irony of the situation and had tongue in cheek when he put pen to paper.

The image of Suzanne or the damsel in distress to be rescued by the politicians is not without appeal,

although looked at more closely, the mathematics (that
is, the proportion of exiting nuns to exiting monks and
the prospects of equal inheritances resolving the spinster predicament, etc.) have an unnerving transparency.
The Assembly, whose real interest in 1790 was to lay
hold of church property without causing undue hardship, and in terms which presented the activity as one
which would promote moral regeneration, demonstrated a stunning ignorance about female religious and
their psychological attributes. According to official statistics, there existed in France in 1789 some eighty thousand religious of whom at least fifty-five thousand were
women, thus making nonsense of the notion of a perfect balance for matrimony.[1] Entry into the male houses
had declined steadily over the century. The expulsion
of the Jesuits in 1764 had removed the most dynamic
force from the male religious life. There remained relatively vital orders such as the Eudistes and the Sale-
sians, both dedicated to the education of boys, but their
numbers too were declining and many of the brothers
when offered a pension and the opportunity to teach
in a lay capacity did not hesitate to grasp them. They
behaved in short as the Assembly had predicted.

The same was not true of the women. Since the seventeenth century, there had been a marked shift in the
emphasis of female religious life away from the contemplative orders (Benedictines, Augustinians) towards
those, many of them the product of post-Tridentine
Catholic social thought, which performed an active social role. This swing was reflected in the age structure
of the contemplative houses where the average age of
the nuns in 1789 was often over fifty. Reintegration
into society through marriage was hardly a likelihood

for most of the women in this age range and all they could hope for was to fill the role of maiden aunt in a brother's dwelling.[2]

The most conspicuous success story of the Counter-Reformation in France is provided by the Sisters of Charity who accounted for more than 15 per cent of all those who appeared in the official count. Devoted largely to the staffing of hospitals for the sick (Hôtels Dieu) or asylums for the old, crippled, and orphaned (Hôpitaux généraux), they and similar orders – for they were not alone but simply the largest – provided France with the best and most effective nursing services in Europe. They covered about two thousand establishments. This was the nursing order which Florence Nightingale struggled seventy years later to emulate. She could not hope to do so so cheaply. The Sisters of Charity worked in exchange for their keep and a modest seventy-five livres a year. The institution they entered put a roof above their heads and each brought into the order a dowry which contributed to her upkeep. Small wonder the Assembly opted for excluding the nursing services from their general dispensations. After several pressing and clearly panic-stricken requests for clarification, it was officially declared that the laws were not directed against congregations.

When they forbade the running of religious schools and pronounced the closure of educational orders, stripping those orders like the Charity at Bayeux who ran orphanages, hospitals, and schools of their last function, the politicians insisted that welfare services were not in jeopardy. Even the Comité de Mendicité was prepared to offer the nursing sisters the ultimate éloge for dedication to hard work. It would, however, have wished to change the style of the Sisters of Charity to that of Citoyennes de Secours. This apparently cosmetic exercise, if the women in question had been willing, would have suited the Assembly wonderfully well. At a stroke, the Catholic element would have ceded to the civic: service to God performed through community service would have yielded to service to the state. The problem was not that the women did not understand the politicians' request but that they understood it too well.

The politicians also believed that on no account should the nursing orders have any control over financial management. The members of the Comité de Mendicité were persuaded that the hôpitaux généraux and the Hôtels Dieu constituted a considerable capital resource which had been conspicuously mismanaged by urban administrators and by the women who ran the hospitals. At every step, the politicians were conscious that there were financial issues to be resolved but hoped to defer ultimate resolution of them until the time when they had more precise information.

The Sisters of Charity was only one of a large number of associations designed to proffer community services. Many such associations were not bound by solemn vows and had escaped claustration. Whereas both the Visitandines and the Ursulines, dedicated to care of the sick and the education of girls, had proved so successful and so attractive to women in the seventeenth century that the Catholic hierarchy had forced solemn vows and claustration upon them, smaller associations, congregations, and communities had avoided both. The members of these communities took 'simple vows' in which they pledged themselves to a specific social role often at a purely local level. The nature of their com-

mitment ranged from help for the domiciled sick, layettes for nursing mothers, provision of shoes for the
young, soup kitchens to cope with dearth, to the teaching of basic literacy or vocational skills to young girls.
Such *filles agrégées* or *associées* were legion and often
specific to a particular locality: hence the Sisters of Saint
Joseph du Puy, the Soeurs Chrétiennes de Nevers, the
Soeurs du Bon Pasteur, the Paulines de Tréguier, the
Dames de la Charité de Laval, etc. Often founded by
a widow or group of widows who endowed the association with their frequently quite modest resources,
these associations might enjoy over the century or so
of their existence no more than local success. They might
have accumulated a little property from donations or
from the dowries or gifts of the women who joined the
association which would permit the members to devote
themselves to their charitable target. Such associations
were not counted in the tally made by the Assembly
– indeed had they been so the number of religious
would have been at least four times greater. The mu-
nicipalities and the districts were not anxious in 1790
to trouble them in their allotted tasks and merely enquired of the Assembly whether or not the new legislation applied to those taking *voeux simples*, which
did not necessarily involve making a lifetime's commitment, or, to avoid an answer they did not wish to
hear, they simply did not mention them at all.

The effect of the legislation abolishing religious vows
did not then result in a massive exodus of nubile Suzannes. Rather, the aged members of dwindling aris-
tocratic contemplative orders largely rejected the offer
to disband since they were unable to conceive of a life
for themselves outside the cloister and they awaited
amalgamation. The Ursulines and the Visitandines lost

their teaching functions but again tried to hang on and find an alternative justification for maintaining a corporate existence. The hospital sisters were instructed to continue. Straddling the terms of the law were huge numbers of women dedicated to charitable work, mostly in small towns and larger villages. Some were widows, some pious spinsters, some *demoiselles* of modest means for whom philanthropy was a way of life and who had an important role to play in village society. There were enough Suzannes in the situation for a couple of them to write letters of thanks to the Assembly for reintegrating them in society, but they constituted something under 1 per cent. However, the legislation boded ill for the future of the religious life. Though their situation was ambiguous, those who stayed on or claimed the law did not apply to them were rendered apprehensive about their fate. They identified themselves with the old regime. In the course of 1790 – 1 as the male secular clergy were pressed to take oaths of loyalty and Catholic social policy came under attack, many, as we shall presently see, became overtly anti-revolutionary. Real nuns and sisters were not dazzled by *les bienfaits de la Révolution*.

Whilst the female religious were becoming aware of their anomalous position in the new France, the Constituent Assembly was under pressure from the Paris authorities to turn its attention to the question of poor relief. It added to its list of standing committees a Comité de Mendicité whose express brief was to formulate a new public assistance policy.[3] The members began with a number of working notions about the problem of poverty. These notions were grounded in enlightenment premises and these included a burning and deep-seated anticlericalism. Dominating their views was the belief that the ready availability of Catholic philanthropy whose justification was the belief that donations to the poor secured the donor a comfortable niche in heaven had created a large group of social parasites. Charity, as dispensed by pious individuals, bureaux de charité, and religious orders was a *pain d'humiliation*. It was also dangerous for it perpetuated the hold of the Catholic church over society. The Comité de Mendicité had a concept both of the Catholic giver and of the recipient of his alms. The giver was locked in superstition. He or she believed that the mere act of giving to the pauper purchased an entrée to a comfortable hereafter. In pursuit of the right of entrance, the giver did not trouble to look too closely at the pernicious effects such putative generosity might have on the recipient. The latter was perceived as the idle father of scrounging children to whom he passed on his attributes. The vocabulary of demanding alms embodied a hypocritical rhetoric in which the word 'god' was ever present. The poor in this view were calculators of the worst kind. They dealt in a spiritual blackmail. However, they were also gamblers. Knowing that they had the fail-safe of Catholic charity at the end of the day, they did not save for the future. Let us remember one of the enlightenment high priests, Montesquieu, who assures us in Book Six of *De l'Esprit des Lois* that he has personally noted that when there is an *hôpital général* in a town, the poor shrug off thoughts of the future with the words *j'irai à l'hospice*. Such spurious empiricism was typical of the armchair philosophers when dealing with the lower orders. The Comité de Mendicité had at its disposal a great deal of statistical matter relative to the existence of relief since there had been a massive enquiry into the financial

status of the hospices as a result of the impending bank-
ruptcies of many of these institutions in the 1760s.[4]
Nevertheless, it clung to the belief that the hospitals
were an uneconomic way of coping with the poor and
that behind them lay considerable and mismanaged
reserves of property and endowments which could be
assumed by the state and put to far better use once the
real poor had been weeded out from the scroungers.
The members were also devotees of the work project
– indeed, they came close to formulating the principle
of the right to work – and they interpreted the work
project as the bedrock of relief to the able-bodied adult
male. They did not deny the existence of a large number
of needy people within France. How many they would
presently discern. They believed, however, that merely
to destroy the existing system must have a salutary
effect provided they could find a fail-safe for the true
poor. Government, or rather good government, was the
key to the situation.

The Comité de Mendicité was populationist. It also
knew that France had a foundling problem because
there existed voluminous records attesting to that fact
and laying claim to government funds to care for these
infants by paying *nourrices* and maintaining orphanages. The numbers of children left anonymously to the
care of society, however, were interpreted as the product of the uncompromising legislation of Henri II. This
legislation obliged the unmarried mother to register her
pregnancy and state the father of the child so that he
could be pursued for its maintenance. If she did not
do so, she ran the risk of the charge of infanticide if
the child was found dead or stillborn.[5] This humiliating
process, the Comité believed, made women turn to
clandestinité to protect themselves and their lovers.

Abolish this piece of legislation, the members argued, and remove the stigma attached to illegitimacy and most women would hold on to their children. Those who needed monetary assistance would receive it from the state and the children who were abandoned would also receive unquestioned subsidy. They would be rebaptized under the generic heading *'enfants de la patrie'* and regarded as a precious human resource of potential soldiers and mothers.[6]

This was the thinking behind what was to be subsequently presented as a charter for the Don Juan and which nineteenth-century French feminists were to strive to undermine by a reimposition of *recherche de la paternité* laws. In the context of the legislative work of the Comité de Mendicité, the seducer was pardoned as human and the seduced assured that she was not degraded by her plight.[7]

An appropriate amount of rhetoric was expended both on the babies and on any family that might receive them. The term *enfant de la patrie* suggested the new valorization of *une classe intéressante* (a euphemism employed for a potentially useful human resource) and the state assumed the role of father. The family that received the child according to the rhetoric provided a state service for which payment and gratitude were due. The child would be reared in the country and would blossom into a dignified citizen since his family would adopt him (with appropriate compensation). The women who suckled these children were referred to in the discourse as *citoyennes précieuses,* and were the only women I know of who were given such a title in the context of the Revolution. They were ennobled by the milk they dispensed – the breast fetishism of the constituents is never far away – because this was giving of themselves to the state. The *nourrice* is in fact often referred to as giving of her blood. The mercenary aspect of her labour is glossed over. She assumes a quasi-mystical role. Indeed one is reminded of the imagery of the pious pelican of the *adoro te* – the one who gave her blood to feed her starving children. Her glory, of course, since she was assumed to be married, reflected on her husband who opened up his hearth to the *enfant de la patrie*.[8]

If any job description was upgraded in 1790 it was certainly that of mercenary wet-nurse. *La précieuse citoyenne* can be placed in our gallery of mythical women of revolutionary rhetoric because the realities of her existence and her de facto valorization by subsequent governments bore no relation to the job description.

The real mercenary wet-nurse of eighteenth-century France who took in an *enfant trouvé* was at the very bottom of the social scale and the job was undertaken because the family in question had no other available recourse such as domestic industry to bring in needful ancillary income. An abandoned child was a risky business. Several carried hereditary syphilis or gonorrhoea and passed the contamination on to the women who suckled them. The speed with which children had to be got to a *nourrice* did not allow the hospitals time to check on their condition and in any case symptoms could be slow to manifest themselves.[9] The risks of taking such a child reflected dire need. I doubt if any woman thought of herself as dispensing *le lait de l'amour de la constitution* or *le lait de la liberté* or indeed any of the rhetorical substances lingered on by the politicians. The baby was a job. This does not convert the mercenary nurse into an automatic murderer of the child she suckled – she had, after all, a vested interest in keeping it alive. It does, however, distinguish our vision of her from that of the politicians.

Let us return to the work of the Comité de Mendicité and its efforts to define anew the poor of France. The members recognized the need for a sound statistical base to enable them to arrive at an estimate of expenditure. These statistics had to define and categorize the poor to make sure they were not scroungers. At the same time, the resources of the hospitals would be assessed. It should be added that the members also hoped that national property would be used to create farms for the landless. The questionnaire designed to inform them about the true poor was far from being a neutral document.[10] The minds of the members of the committee were not tabulae rasae. They embarked with a large number of preconceptions which had an impact upon the results they were to receive. Fundamental to their logic was the belief that the family was the primary unit upon which all society was based. A family endowed its head with certain responsibilities which included the rent of an appropriate shelter and the feeding of the young until they could labour in their own support. It was assumed, and the assumption was confirmed in debate, that an adult man and wife could, if dependent on wage labour, support themselves and two children – presumed to be their replacements in the population. However, with the advent of a third child, such a family, it was also assumed, would need a subvention. Clearly a father could fall ill or die or experience periods of unemployment. The sick poor of either sex had claims to subvention as did the old past work. Unemployment could only be remedied by job creation – work on the roads was the first thought. Such work would have to be unskilled since the variety of

people seeking it would make anything else problematic.

The Comité therefore applied a logic to its deliberations and the formulation of its questionnaire which
begged a number of vital issues. The first was that of
the adequacy of the wage to do what it was assumed
it did. The members spent a great deal of time and
energy in trying to work out exactly how much a man
and his wife should earn in order to support two children. They appear to have abandoned this effort.[11] The
Comité was very afraid of being involved in disputes
about the level of wages. It was totally resistant to claims
that wage levels in a particular sector were inadequate
to sustain even a small family. The Loi Chapelier which
was to resist the right of association to push up wage
levels is wholeheartedly endorsed in its debates. The
equality of the Revolution was, after all, the equality
of the free market economy.

This was a serious consideration but it has particular
force with respect to women. The wage levels they
could command on the open market were about a third,
in rare cases half, those of men. They precluded an
independent existence because although they might
provide a woman with enough to eat and clothe herself,
they certainly would not put a roof above her head or
purchase fuel.[12] A woman could not on her wages support a child in widowhood. The woman alone in this
society, irrespective of the state of her physical health
or her age, could at any moment find herself in dire
economic straits. About 14 per cent of the age cohorts
born in the second half of the eighteenth century were
permanent spinsters and perhaps as much as 90 per
cent of them were below the basic poverty line if we
define that line as demarcating the ability to be fed,

warm and sheltered. Yet the questionnaire did not want to know about them.

The questionnaire also ran into difficulties over the question of the smallholder and his family. In some regions, over 80 per cent of holdings were inadequate for the maintenance of a family and the family was dependent upon a multiplicity of expedients to sustain life ranging from seasonal migration to domestic industry in the dead season and begging or putting one's children out to beg. Work projects such as demolition work or work on the roads might be impossible in mountain villages in the winter when an extra income was needed. A further problem was that of the industrial family. The cotton and woollen industries of northern France on the eve of the Revolution were in deeply troubled times. The layoffs were particularly acute amongst spinners.[13] Most of the married women had smallholders for husbands but the viability of the family economy depended upon female labour. The drying up of that source reduced entire communities to beggary. Yet the fact that the husbands were not strictly out of work precluded their consideration for assistance under the rubric of the Comité's questionnaire. The stolid rejection of the idea of accepting the inadequacy of a wage to support a worker – particularly a female worker – in fact ensured that the statistics of the Comité were a considerable under-recording of the problem of poverty in some areas. Indeed, the failure of many smallholding areas to reply to it reflected the appreciation by local district officials of its lack of relevance to their particular situation. Yet, ironically, the Comité was to insist that the districts had exaggerated the numbers of those in need of relief by failing to observe its criteria of no help for families of under three children and by including the seasonally unemployed as full paupers.

Why did it do this? The sum of money voted by the Constituent for the subvention of the poor was far less than had been hoped for and the number of poor returned by the districts was greater than envisaged. The sum covered only a fraction of the Comité's estimates which in any case were an under-reading of the situation. Faced with admitting that they had laboured for nothing and had been virtually ignored by the Assembly, they chose instead to save face by saying that the districts had lied and that in making available funds for a number of work projects and for the sick hospitalized poor, they had resolved the problem of poverty.[14]

There are many historians who have lauded the work of the Constituent Assembly as the truly creative aspect of the Revolution before its deals were jeopardized by war and Terror.[15] Its policies for dealing with the poor have been assumed to be a logical and fair substitute for the frequently messy and certainly random practices of ancien régime Catholic society. A closer examination, however, shows the plans to be structurally flawed and, even supposing they had been fully implemented, it is seriously to be questioned whether they would have provided any more effective relief to the poor than the mixture of Catholic philanthropy and state and private subsidies which had previously existed.[16] Historians have perhaps too readily accepted that the plans of 1790–1 were an improvement on the random system previously pertaining and were systematic and egalitarian. In fact, the situation in 1791 when the Constituent Assembly wound itself up was to say the least messy. It had suspended religious vows and put the

personnel of the hospital on a temporary footing pend-
ing further consideration of the staffing of the hospitals. It had assumed the funding of the hospitals but
had suspended absorption of their property as *biens
nationaux*; it had taken on the burden of the *enfants
trouvés* which it had assumed would diminish as illegitimacy lost some of its social stigma; it had decried
and sought the structural demolition of the traditional
ways of according relief under the old regime and had
emasculated the role of the curé as arbiter or orchestrator of parish funds. It had formulated principles of
poor relief which begged the whole issue of the adequacy of the wage – and the female wage in particular
– to support an individual and dependents and had
discredited its own findings rather than admit that the
state did not proffer adequate funds to realize its limited
objectives. Caught up in all this were the lives of some-
where between one-tenth and one-fifteenth of the total
population.

Critical to an understanding of this demolition process was that it involved the destruction or jeopardy of
an entire set of highly complex female networks. These
included the female world of ritual help which included
nurses and associations to help and organize the needy
and cope with periods of difficulty – however inadequately – on the one hand. The modern analogy would
perhaps be taking Mother Theresa off the streets of
Calcutta. On the other hand these networks were critical in maintaining the delicate balance of the economy
of expedients which sustained many families. I mean
by this the carefully aggregated income sources which
could embody jobs, handouts, and organized begging.
In this 'economy of makeshifts'[17] the mother of a family was the pivot for obvious reasons.

The full impact of change was not experienced overnight. Local administrators in particular were anxious
to protract, if possible, welfare services and some of
the earliest women's clubs were in fact aimed at providing philanthropic services placed at risk by the
changes implicit in the social legislation of the Constituent. They were probably composed of much the
same sort of people who had been concerned with such
work under the old regime. Two factors, however, in
1791–2 were to hasten the demolition process of wom-
en's orders still further. The first might be summarized
as 'Suzanne's perfidy' and the second as the fortunes
of war or the failure of Rousseau's Sophie, daughter
of the enlightened Revolution, to put service to the state
before other concerns.

'Suzanne's perfidy,' the failure of the real nun to
conform to the Assembly's model, went beyond the
mere refusal of women in the religious life to disband
as the Assembly thought they should and involved a
fervent and stolid support of the nonjuring priesthood.
This found expression in the women making available
to the nonjurors convent and hospital chapels for the
saying of mass, thus robbing the constitutional priesthood of its clientèle. Furthermore, the nursing sisters
were in command of the dying and this meant they
determined who administered the last rites and performed burial services. For the sisters who tended the
sick, preparation for a decent Christian burial had always been an important part of their perceived function
and making ready the soul to meet its maker had fig-
ured conspicuously in the discipline which they had
enforced upon themselves and their patients. In the
closing decades of the old regime, the sisters had con-
tested the claims of surgeons and their pupils to per-

form autopsies on corpses or to dismember them to promote anatomical knowledge.[18] The populace saw the sisters as their allies in resisting post mortem mutilation which conflicted with popular notions of the importance of the integrity of the body in the hereafter. The sisters' own deaths were carefully considered in their *règles* (rules of foundation) and specifications for their funeral and burial arrangements were embodied in the contracts which they made with the municipal authorities when they were invited to serve the sick poor of the hospitals. In the contracts of the Sisters of Charity, for example, it was laid down: 'in the case of the death of any of the said sisters it will be borne in mind that she died in the service of the poor: it will be permitted to the other sisters to bury the corpse of the deceased, each one holding a candle in her hand; and after the celebration of one high and two low masses, the body of the deceased will be buried in the church or cemetery of the said hospital.'[19]

To deny the sisters control over their own funerals was to break their contracts.[20] Similarly, written into the sisters' contracts was the right to nominate their confessor. To intrude in this right was again to breach the contract. However, and this was the source of much contention, many sought to exercise this right by choosing to persist with a non-juror (one who had not taken an oath of loyalty to the state as not merely their own confessor but the one called upon to administer the last rites to the dying). In clinging to their specified confessor, they were capable of questioning the legality and competence of the constitutional priest in the eyes of God to perform in areas critical to the Catholic faith. The challenge presented to the constitutional priest was damaging to his entire status. If he lost control of death

in the parish then he suffered a conspicuous emasculation and was deeply resentful. Furthermore, the hospital chapel proffered the possibility of an alternative
mass to the official one he performed. He might, and
in many cases did, have the humiliation of celebrating
before a virtually empty church whilst the hospital
chapel was full of his parishioners.[21] This situation had
the effect of stripping the sisters of the support of the
new state church.

The increasing association in the context of war of
the nonjurors with treason, the mounting anticlericalism in government circles, coupled with the desire to
evade the financing of two sets of clerics, one of whom
expressed no loyalty to the state, redounded on the
nuns and the female religious who supported the nonjuring church. Several were the victims of reprisals,
window breaking, insults such as the famous flagellation scene in Paris of the offending nuns by *les dames
de la Halle*. In the summer of 1792, the Sisters of Charity in Paris were driven from their main house in Paris
at bayonet point. This incident was the culmination of
a literal hate campaign against the women conducted
in the press by the journalist Gorsas and perhaps most
strikingly in the pages of the *Père Duchêsne*. The last
embarked upon the strategy of encouraging women to
bring other women into line to ensure the patriotism
of the sex. Such an approach has some interest because
it reflects traditional beliefs that much of women's behaviour should be regulated either by the husband or
by the women of the community. Clearly sisters had
no husbands to recall them to their duties or to answer
for them before the courts and hence other women
must call them to account. Brooms were used. A captured sister, one who dared to leave the house, was

pinned down whilst her skirts were raised and the broom used to beat her on the naked buttocks. Not only was the victim humiliated by the exposure of her private parts to a jeering audience – which could be mixed – but the gutter press thereafter commented on the personal physical attributes of her anatomy, often presented to suggest they were typical of her entire order. The gutter press was obviously intent upon cheap laughs but behind the laughter was the recognition that women should not be allowed to defy the state.[22] These examples had some provincial repercussions.

Such incidents did prompt several women to re-examine their role as members of a congregation. Individual Sisters of Charity decided that the job had to come first and religious affiliation was postponed until happier times. Some did, as they were urged by the Assembly, take the title of *citoyennes de secours*, abandoning a garb which was too distinctive and simply getting on with the job.

The number of *contre-révolutionnaires pieuses*, however, was multiplying. When war began in the Vendée in 1792, the houses of the Filles de Sagesse, a congregation which had devoted itself to tending the rural sick since the beginning of the century, became legendary hotbeds of disaffection. Here visions of the Virgin and putative miracles were recorded. Michelet summoned his strongest descriptive powers: 'the Virgin preferred appearing in La Vendée, amongst fogs, thick woods and impenetrable hedges. She profited by the old local superstitions and showed herself in three different places, always near an old druid oak. Her favourite place was the Saint Laurent, where the Filles de Sagesse retailed the miracles, the call for blood.'[23] This congregation became earmarked for official condemnation and produced some notable martyrs during the Revolution. Elsewhere from the autumn of 1793 and with no regular pattern, particular houses of *congréganistes* came under attack. In actual assaults on houses, rather than on individuals, gangs of youths were usually involved. These gangs did not spare *congréganistes* who were known supporters of the nonjuring priesthood. The Sisters of Saint Joseph du Puy, for example, who made no bones about their hostility to the legislation, experienced severe threats to person and property in some of the bourgs of the Haute Loire. Windows were smashed and tiles torn off roofs and tethered animals released. However, the smaller establishments seem to have borne the brunt of the attack and the mother house was spared.

In the country 1792–3 saw an increasing number of sisters forced to disband, merging into village society or returning to their families of origin. Many had to try to earn a living and were given shelter by sympathetic friends or relatives. Some clearly tried to continue service to the community like the above-cited Sisters of Saint Joseph du Puy, many of whom split up and became known as *les filles à carreau* – daughters of the lace pillow – who sought to make a living as lacemakers but served as doctor and nurse to the village that gave them shelter. Many undertook a new spiritual mission, the perpetuation of a fortress faith, and this often involved the organization of clandestine masses offered by a nonjuring priesthood which emerged from hiding at a sign given by the relevant sister who had at her disposal means of alerting the faithful to summon them at an appointed hour to a barn or discreet farmhouse.

This disaffected mass of woman power was technically beyond the law until September 1793 when the

congregations were abolished.[24] Abolition came because the government interpreted them as a dissident
and suspect force and was not prepared to acknowledge the value of the services the women proffered
free to the community. At that point local urban zealots
at war with a countryside which resisted dechristianization and price fixation moved into an attack on the
filles associées whom it saw as the main force behind
the disaffection of many villages. Such officials exceeded the letter of the law by demanding of the women
an oath of loyalty. Imprisonments began. The *sub rosa*
activities of the village might be scrutinized and the
female religious at liberty had no choice but to keep
their heads down.

Away from the main towns and in areas where officialdom did not pry too closely many female religious
became the crucial elements in the organization of a
fortress faith. This touches upon an aspect of the religious experience of the villages during the Revolution
which demands more attention from historians. The
congréganistes were known in the villages and respected
for the work they did with the poor and disadvantaged.
Some had run *petites écoles* (winter schools) in the villages which had given village women such literacy as
they possessed and often, in addition, sewing and industrial skills specific to certain regions such as lacemaking in the Velay or in Normandy. When they
returned home they dedicated themselves full time to
a particular kind of subversive activity, laying away the
dead, teaching the catechism, reading the Bible, and
reciting the rosary, and as the dechristianizing process
developed apace in 1794, they took the lead in priest
sheltering and the organization of clandestine masses.
They divided up the priest's vestments and the holy

vessels amongst the village women so that no one ran the risk of being found with substantial evidence to prove her guilty in their possession. They used small children as their messengers to alert the people as to when the priest would appear. Finally, when they knew of a priest in hiding, they regulated his public appearances perhaps even to the point, as Michelet insists, of forcing him to take the risk of appearing in public to say mass. After June 1792, such activity could entail real danger for the priests who had refused an oath of loyalty to the state. Many of them were elderly or frail and sought the security of anonymity only to find themselves forced to emerge periodically from hiding to fulfil the expectations of those who sheltered them.

Let us leave for the moment 'Suzanne's perfidy,' her dogged refusal to be grateful to the politicians and to toe the line, and concentrate on the fortunes of war which caused a new definition of those who might make demands upon the public purse. Mounting inflation and the cost of maintaining a war on two frontiers clearly strained the budget of the French state. In assuming the responsibility for the relief of the poor, the state had taken upon itself an immense burden. The question was: could it sustain that burden?

With the advantage of hindsight and our consciousness of the close relationship between economic growth, population levels, and the capacity of a state to provide even at the most basic level for the needs of those of its citizenry dependent on the work of their hands or disadvantaged by age or debility, we now appreciate that revolutionary France was overambitious in believing that it could effectively subvent up to a fifth of its citizenry. Its ability to do so in the context of war and spiralling inflation became doubly problematic. Yet, as its capacity to provide the means for an effective state welfare program receded, the political rhetoric denouncing traditional charity and even the idea of the hospital intensified amongst the politicians. Almsgiving of any kind was prohibited by the law of 24 vendemiaire year II (16 October 1794). *Bienfaisance* (philanthropy), it was insisted, was not doing good when performed by an individual who appeased only his own inherent vanity and his desire to exercise power over the recipient. The hospitals with their hundred thousand old people, orphaned, and handicapped appeared in the rhetoric as punitive institutions designed to oppress the afflicted. Close them and put their inmates back in their homes. Whether or not such homes existed was not discussed.

Legislation passed in March and June 1794 extolled the desirability of home relief and promised state pensions to the rural poor whose names were to be recorded in a *Grand Livre de Bienfaisance Nationale*. This legislation was followed by the law of 23 messidor year II (11 July 1794) sanctioning the nationalization of hospital property and promising the redistribution of the property of political suspects among indigent patriots.

Did the politicians know what they were doing or were they the victims of their own rhetoric? Were the promises cost cutting in disguise? The discourse on the deserving poor established priorities. The war wounded and their families were to have first demands upon the resources of the state. Invalidity pensions for wounded soldiers were increased and the ordinary soldier was given parity with the officer: the needy families of *défenseurs de la patrie* were promised more help under legislation of pluviose year II. Pensions to war widows were increased and allegedly made easier to obtain by

a law of 13 prairial year II (1 June 1794). Consideration
for the war wounded demanded further thought about
the abolition of the hospitals.

The package designed to care for the war wounded
and their families and the promises of relief to the rural
needy look impressive but they were all subject to conspicuous underfunding and delays. So pessimistic were
local authorities, stretched to their utmost with subsistence problems, that less than a fifth of the districts
submitted a *livre de bienfaisance*. The pensions for war
wounded and soldiers' widows caused universal complaint. Every branch of public assistance was months
in arrears.

Delays and then the suspension of funding had dire
repercussions on the hospitals. Although perhaps a majority of departments hung back rather than put hospital property on the market in order to keep them
running, some funding was needed. If the departments
were to keep the buildings open they needed some
personnel. In the course of the debates on the care of
the sick the politicians had had some remarks to make
on a paid nursing force which demonstrated the degree
to which nursing services were undervalorized but also
provides us with another set of mythical people who
were the figment of political rhetoric.

The politicians in debating whether or not the mercenary nurse was a necessity alluded to women under
the generic heading of *'nos filles'* – our daughters. *'Nos
filles'* were not the daughters of anyone in particular.
There is no reason to suppose that they were the
daughters of the politicians. They were perhaps intended to be the daughters of France. They were certainly someone else's daughters. The discourse
distinguished between them and *'les filles'* such as les

Filles de la Charité for whom tending of the poor was seen as a God-given role. *'Nos filles'* were putative young women who allowed certain natural attributes of womanhood to surface. These attributes were not mercenary. 'Everyone knows,' said one deputy 'that *nos filles* know how to tend the sick and old. Nature provides the capacity. These are not taught skills. *Nos filles* tend us in our homes and they do not expect payment. Surely they can do the same for free for the Republic?

Such sentiments, in the context of a money-saving exercise, were not the cause of violent dissent. *La bonté naturelle de nos filles* could save France on the nursing front and money could be forgotten. They would of course proffer their administrations within their homes.

There is no record of which I am aware which shows a politician sacrificing his daughter to the hospices of France or indeed sending them into the homes of the poor. The eighteenth-century hospital was essentially a place for the suffering poor, the dirty, the diseased, and the underfed. It also served the military and in the context of war this aspect of the business could only increase. Standards could only be maintained by a strict discipline. The protection of a uniform, as Miss Nightingale realized, carried with it a measure of authority. Middle-class women, unless motivated by an unquenchable spiritual flame, were unlikely to take on demanding labour which exposed them to the diseased male torso and the unbridled male tongue. Sophie, as Rousseau insisted, must have a conspicuously delicate disposition, a pleasing modesty. She could not be exposed to the moral dangers of contact with the military if Emile was to rest easy about the legitimacy of his progeny. Nursing service could not be this particular Sophie's choice.

The only women who could be lured to work as replacements for the religious in the hospitals were working-class women who needed the money to survive. Far from drawing upon the inherent bounty natural to the politicians' imagery of *'nos filles,'* and lacking the dedication of *'les filles'* (or women in the religious life) when money failed to materialize to pay their wages, the mercenary nurses stripped the beds of sheets from under the sick and carried off the bowls, cutlery, and anything else they could lay their hands on.[25] From 1793, the hospitals survived only in the most nominal sense and those which did so with the most success were those where a nursing sister of the old regime was prepared to continue and put commitment to the sick before her commitment to the Catholic church and where local fundraising (the voluntary or involuntary charity decried by the politicians) provided some substitute for the funds which the government neither could nor would supply.

Whether or not the nursing sisters were driven from the hospitals depended on two factors: first, the degree to which local administrators were prepared to put the interests of the patients in the institution before a doctrinaire commitment to dismissing the sisters, and second, which profile the sisters themselves were prepared to adopt. If sisters were prepared to continue to work and sacrifice their distinctive garb which drew attention to them, to keep their heads down and renounce counter-revolutionary activity such as priest sheltering, then they could survive. Hence the Sisters of Charity though expelled in Paris were retained at Montpellier. The nursing sisters were suspended and imprisoned at Le Puy but not at Mende across the hills. An active *société populaire* or an overzealous *représentant en mis-*

sion could mean an unwelcome intrusion in the functioning of the hospitals. Probably most local officials, unless prompted by the *sociétés populaires* or the *représentants en mission*, did their utmost to keep a hospital going and to retain the services of the nursing sisters. Where they could not do so, an effort to reinstate them was an early priority after thermidor.[26]

Early victims of government commitment to the war effort were *les citoyennes précieuses* and *les enfants de la patrie*. In the context of dearth, war, massive layoffs in female employment, and domestic strife, the numbers of foundlings trebled and quadrupled. The quite generous payments made initially to the mercenary wet-nurses were the same in the year VIII in spite of the vicissitudes of the currency. Worse still, by the year III, delays of up to fourteen months were reported in payment, with the districts passing on any delay in government funding to the nurses. For the next six years, a huge gap existed between the official offering salary and what could be realized in any one year. Arrears were never fully paid.[27]

The chronicle of the results of government defaulting takes the form of a grim necrology. A tally of the deaths of the children administered by the hospital of Rouen shows that whilst the numbers of infants doubled and trebled, the death rate rose from 70 to 95 per cent and above between 1793 and the year V.[28]

The necrology, however, is not a simple one. It is accompanied by a starkly dramatic commentary.

Weary of the futile promises of administrators, the wet-nurses have notified the hospitals of their intention to return the children if payment is not made.
(Saint Gaudens an V)[29]

They are reduced to beg from charitable people and share
the little they can raise with their foster children.
(Bellesme Orne an v)[30]

Total despair amongst the local wet-nurses who have
made a collective return of children they have maintained
for two years without payment. Women and children are
starving ... (Domfront an v)[31]

Most administrators insisted that if a woman already
had a foster child, she thought twice before returning
it to the hospital where death was certain. In any case,
they had some cards with which to blackmail the
woman. First, they insisted that when the money did
come, only women who had a child at that moment
would be paid promptly. They urged women to take
on a second child if one died to ensure continuity of
payment, and to breast-feed more than one child –
indeed there was no limit on the numbers one might
take on – in order to secure priority payment when the
money came. None of these policies had any long-term
effect given the penury of the level of the population
to which these women belonged. Given also the relationship between nutritional levels and the ability to
breast-feed a child and the evidence of amenorrhoea
amongst the women of the working classes of northern
France after the dearth of the years III and IV, nature
– if not the kind in which the rhetoric of the Enlightenment indulged – grimly resolved the plight of many
mothers and babies. Where the mortality rate was not
100 per cent amongst *les enfants de la patrie*, tribute
should be made to *les précieuses citoyennes*, those with
nothing to sell but their milk. They remain the only

explanation of why the entire foundling population was not annihilated.

The greatest claims for the long-term efficacy of revolutionary assistance have been made for the city of Paris.[32]Here a number of *comités de bienfaisance* were set up in the sections intended to provide relief at home to the domiciled poor. They embarked with high hopes of a system coordinated by 'a rotating company of respectable citizens freely elected,' survived the early days of a power struggle with the municipality which was prepared to rely more heavily on clerical help, and then passed under the direction (March 1793) of the Commission centrale de bienfaisance which was made up of an unsalaried member from each of the sectional *comités*. It had the task of allocating such funds as were to be had to the sections according to the size of their indigent population. The *comités de bienfaisance* form a very interesting area of study because they demonstrate how the doctrinaire approach of the Convention and its prioritization of limited categories of indigent were modified at the sectional level. Though directed by unsalaried mature male citizens of distinctly bourgeois status, the actual work of visiting the domiciled poor would seem to have been left to women accorded 'adjunct' status. The rhetoric employed by the *comité* of the Champs Elysées sounds strikingly similar to that used by old regime bishops when extolling the *congréganistes*: 'It is up to you *citoyennes* to assuage severity and to present the situation and needs of those who ask our assistance in its true light ... it is impossible for us to do this without you. Men ... are afraid to face the unfortunate and they avert their gaze from their suffering. Women alone have the courage to stare at need without flinching and can evaluate its extent.'[33] In other words, the hovels of the poor were left to the woman visitor. In some sections women were enlisted to visit the pregnant and to make free layettes and prepare bedding for nursing mothers. What one would like to know is how many of the women visitors had previous experience of the same kind of work under the old regime? Certainly, individual Sisters of Charity, cosmetically changed to *citoyennes de secours*, were retained to run soup kitchens. The *comités* recognized three categories of poor: the elderly and infirm, pregnant women and nursing mothers who could not work, and 'those responsible for the support of a family whose indigence is temporary.' There was certainly a sensitivity to the special plight of working women conspicuously absent at the national level.

There are many citizens of both sexes in the sections who, although they are not numbered amongst those who have benefitted from the benificence of the Convention ... nonetheless have the same need for assistance ... Such are the workers and artisans of all types, the day labourers and the women whose entire income consists of the modest product of their labour, which scarcely suffices for the subsistence of themselves and their children and who in hard times, or in case of illness or temporary incapacity, require subsidies proportionate to their needs.[34]

In their appreciation of who were the poor the comités de bienfaisance were exemplary and demonstrate an understanding unequalled in official circles. In the event, however, they were unable to find sufficient funding, and help by September 1794 barely covered the sick. Moreover, private philanthropy, in the form of specific donations by private individuals, privileges such as a surcharge of 4 per cent on the sale of butter and eggs at market and door-to-door collections on much the same principle as the *quêtes* of the old regime progressively became the main source of any continuing help. France did not lose its philanthropic instinct during the revolutionary years though it is hard to know how many donations were made under duress.[35]

When on 23 messidor year II (11 July 1794) all charitable endowments were declared nationalized and the *commission centrale* had to justify expenditure before receipt of funds, total crisis ensued. Small wonder the suffering old demanded hospitals to end their days.

Like the *bureaux de charité* of the old regime the comités de bienfaisance struggled on but there were months when the only distribution to the poor was of four potatoes per head. This was no panacea for the hardships of 1794–5.

The Revolution was not responsible for the dearth of the years III and IV, yet this phenomenon revealed, more than anything else could have done, the barrenness of a welfare system that had no existence in anything other than the rhetoric of the politicians. Without the war, the chaos might have been less and a number of innocent victims spared, but the very premises of the work of the Comité de Mendicité and the inadequacy of state funding – even in a peacetime context – to cope with the problem of poverty in French society would still have produced both dislocation and ill feeling. The slump in textile production which had begun in the last decade of the old regime was exacerbated by the reduced purchasing power of the masses in the context of inflation and war and by the decline in the production of luxury goods such as lace and velvet and ephemera which only the re-emergence of a court civilization under Napoleon could go some way to reinvigorate. The fall in the French birth rate visible after 1796 can be attributed to the postponement of marriage by the young who were caught in an economic trap. Soldiers, apprentices, and maidservants whose wages were paid retroactively or in assignats which bore no relationship to their face value hesitated before tying permanent knots. Amenorrhoea in 1795–6 in Northern France may also have been a contributory factor. The female body is a singularly grim metering device for degrees of deprivation.

The Revolution was not a neutral commodity whose effects were optional for those who lived through it. When Richard Cobb reminded us that the unmarried girl who was impregnated on 9 thermidor by a lover who abandoned her would not remember the date as that of the fall of Robespierre he spoke a kind of truth.[36] Yet, as a Parisian, she would have felt the reduction in the amount of bread which she experienced in the year III and the child she bore would have stood a better chance of survival if the politicians had demonstrated a firmer commitment to the *citoyennes précieuses*.

The spoliation of the hospitals, the reduction or loss of the nursing sisters, the dispersal of the congréganistes, the stripping of the villages of their traditional means of support, however inadequate this might have been, became part of a revolutionary experience which ingrained itself on popular memory. In 1816 the mayor of Toulouse is said to have brought a large demonstration against food shortages to an end with the words 'voulez-vous la charité des philosophes.' It was a euphemism for high-sounding promises with no backing.

The victims of the rhetoric were the hungry, the sick, the old, and the little *enfants de la patrie*, the last privileged in the sense that their early deaths spared them further suffering.

The people were not fools. Collectively and individually, the Revolution provided them with a set of experiences. If the poor suffered above all, this fact did not remain unnoticed by those women who had in some instances dedicated their lives to good works and who had not only experienced the demolition process at first hand but had in some cases suffered for their previous commitment to a form of charity decried as pernicious by the men of 1789. As Terror released its grip and confronted with evident immiseration many would mobilize afresh. Their spirit of mission would exceed even the heady days of the Catholic Counter-Reformation.

CHAPTER THREE

In Search of Counter-Revolutionary Women

In Search of Counter-Revolutionary Women

The earlier description of the women of Paris between the October Days and Germinal insisted upon the presence of extremes of emotion: the gradual replacement of hope, excitement, and belief in the Revolution by disillusionment, fear, and a sense of betrayal. Intensity of emotion during the Revolution was not the monopoly of the capital. The constituent elements, however, of the emotional response of women outside Paris to the momentous changes taking place around them were different. In no city other than Paris could women feel they had been so instrumental in forcing the pace of political life. In some the Revolution was undoubtedly born in hope. However, right from the beginning, many towns, like Bayeux in Normandy, were very exposed to hardship from the changes of the Revolution because their economy was threatened by the disappearance of

ancien régime institutions or they were involved in economic activities which stagnated in a slump generated
or enhanced by the Revolution.

A good economic history of the French Revolution
which takes a closer look at women's role in proto-
industry remains to be written.[1] What can be proffered
as a generalization is that textile production in the
eighteenth century drew upon a huge reservoir of cheap
female labour and that rural outwork by women was
the means whereby many smallholdings were buttressed and a viable family economy made possible.

Furthermore, industrial slump, already advanced
throughout France on the eve of the Revolution, continued until after the restoration to be particularly acute
in luxury industries. The fine silk and velvet of international renown, whose production centred on Lyons,
Nimes, and Tours, the manufacture of ribbons and em-
broideries in the villages around Saint Etienne, the knitting of fine, white cotton stockings in Brittany and
Normandy, the glove-making industries of Millau, and
the button-making which took place in many villages
of the Ile de France were all labour intensive and 90
per cent and upwards of the workforce were women.[2]

The lace industry was in the hands of women through
every stage of production and sale and employed lit-
erally thousands of women in the Pays de Velay, in
Lower Normandy and around Alençon, and of course
in Chantilly whose associations with Madame de Pom-
padour excited hostility to the workforce in 1790 when
the women were stoned by a crowd – one whose composition has never been analyzed. Lace production virtually ceased during the Revolution and did not pick
up again until Napoleon made conspicuous consump-
tion the order of the day at court. Families which lost

the input into the household economy of a working mother could expect, as we have seen, no substitute assistance. They had no claims upon whatever relief there was to be had. Need we be surprised that women were quick to associate the Revolution with increasing immiseration? Indeed, there may even have been an industry-specific response in which specialized work-forces, as at Lyons, became the earliest critics of the Revolution.[3]

Price fixation was perhaps the most socially divisive piece of revolutionary legislation, a fact not lost on the Jacobins who resisted as long as they could the aban-donment of laissez-faire. Townspeople needed no per-suasion to associate their problems in securing grain with peasant chicanery. They believed the peasant in-volved in plots to withhold grain to beat the maximum and in the operation of a black market. The maximum worked most efficiently in the big town where admin-istrators feared insurrection and hence were prepared to put coercion behind attempts to bring grain into the city markets. The inhabitants of smaller towns knew their interests to be a low priority. In such small towns, particularly within the Paris provisioning zone, there was a clear perception amongst the masses that they were being deprived to keep the great gaping mouth of the capital filled. In such towns, resentment surfaced as early as 1792. Even if there had been an endorse-ment of the Revolution in its early stages, enthusiasm became disillusionment as the Revolution made in-creasing demands in terms of men and money upon the populace. Long before the maximum was abol-ished, indeed, quite commonly from April 1794, we find food queues forming. Complaints against short-ages and bread riots were common, often marked by

criticism of government and idealization of the old regime. When the women of Bayeux in April of 1794
attacked and stormed the cathedral which had been
turned into an emergency grain store and which also
housed the *société populaire*, they smashed the bust of
Rousseau and screamed 'à bas putain, quand le bon
Dieu était là nous avions du pain' and this at the height
of the dechristianizing campaign.[4]

The Revolution, as we have noted, was not an optional experience to be embraced or rejected at will.
Historians still search for the village which emerged
totally unscathed by events. The bulk of French people
were, of course, peasants. They lived in scattered hamlets or nuclear villages. They did not have the opportunity to participate in anything approaching a
revolutionary *journée* but as taxpayers and suppliers of
cannon fodder, they were called upon to defend the
Revolution against its enemies. It was also unlikely that
they would escape the excesses of Parisian or city revolutionary zeal. The peasant woman, however, has been
somewhat neglected by historians of both sexes. This
is unfortunate because, arguably, the response of this
woman to the Revolution is critical.

We meet her only fleetingly in the history of the
Revolution before 1795. She emerges here and there
from as early as 1790–1 as the target of minor urban
demonstrations in the market for her refusal to surrender milk, cheese, and eggs for assignats, in demonstrations to try to prevent the sale of common land
and the abolition of traditional rights of gleaning and
harvesting which were often an important part of the
family economy of many peasant households. Above
all, from 1791, she moves into the defence of traditional
religion and its priesthood. In so doing, this woman is

transformed little by little into a counter-revolutionary and in due course becomes part of the counter-revolution with a distinctive role to play.

During the bicentenary, an event which above all celebrated discourse and the use of terms, there was considerable debate on what should be considered counter-revolutionary and what anti-revolutionary. Such fine distinctions were not applied by contemporaries who used the term counter-revolutionary as they did aristocrat with a conspicuous generosity and contempt for precision. Even Jacques Roux, the militant of militants, was a counter-revolutionary in the mouths of the Jacobins. The women who are the concern here and were designated counter-revolutionary in the reports of police and government officials were not like the *chouans* those who took to the woods to make war on the Republic or who sought to establish an unmodified ancien régime or even those who in the cause of the White Terror were ready to dismember the bodies of former Jacobin officials. They were more modest personnages who were prepared to turn their backs on the national line. Women who boycotted the mass of the constitutional priest, who in the hard years of 1793–4 organized clandestine masses, who continued to slap a cross on the forehead of the newborn, who placed a Marian girdle on the stomach of the parturient, and who gathered to say the rosary and taught their children their prayers were all committing counter-revolutionary offences. These women did not name their children after Marat. They continued to hallow a pantheon of saints in the way they had always done. If their husbands elected to buy favour by honouring a local official in the naming of their offspring, they slipped a saint's name on as well. They did not when they breast-fed their children reflect that they were endowing them with sound revolutionary principles and a hatred of aristocrats. They resented the décadi which destroyed traditional sociability patterns. They buried their relatives secretly at the dead of night. They probably encouraged their sons to defect and they certainly did not send their children to state schools. Unlike revolutionary woman who was a product of the big cities and the revolutionary *journées* and who had her heyday in 1793 and can be thought about as an architect of the Revolution and as deeply committed to the triumph of popular sovereignty, counter-revolutionary woman evolved slowly. She surfaced in the countryside, in some areas sooner than others, or in the small town which knew it was not a priority in the government's provisioning schemes. She began to win after 1795 though the victory was far from absolute or clear cut. Ultimately, however, she could claim to have made a significant contribution to the reversal of the national record. She nullified all attempts by the Directory to re-establish the rule of law by setting at nought its attempts to tolerate a Catholicism which would pronounce its loyalty to the state and by rendering null its attempts through a state-based civic education to create citizens in a patriotic mould, emancipated from the preconceptions of the past. Against change she posited tradition. She gave practical expression to a dicton existing in many provincial patois: 'Les hommes font les lois; les femmes les traditions.'[5]

This is the woman in Revolution whose spectre will haunt the politicians of the nineteenth century and serve to confirm them in their efforts to deny women the vote. Certainly, this woman has significance in the history of the Roman Catholic Church for it is her commitment to her religion which determines in the post-thermidorean period the re-emergence of the Catholic church on very particular terms, which included an express rejection of state attempts to control a priest-hood and the form of public worship. Counter-revolutionary woman is therefore of consequence in the ongoing religious and political history of France.

Who was she and how does one find out about her? Richard Cobb was able to re-create the *sans-culotte* from his utterings and voluble disquisitions in the *sociétés populaire*, in the sections, and in police reports: a revolutionary man emerged clearly from his utterings. Such a direct re-creation of counter-revolutionary woman is impossible. When she speaks it is through the official who recounts her misdeeds and such officials, as Cobb reminded us in his study *The Police and the People*, were not dispassionate or innocent reporters. Cobb pointed out that an official report was written with an eye to impressing one's superiors if the official wanted to advance in state service. Objectivity was a low priority when promotion was the official's desideratum.[6] In short, any text we are proffered from this type of source needs careful scrutiny, not least when an official recounts his dealings with women and is conscious that his comportment may be judged according to different criteria from those used if he were dealing with men.

When officials encountered women and described their floutings of the law to their superiors, they might, in order to maintain their own image, proffer a distorted version to preserve their own reputation. For example, the description of a local response to the inauguration of the feast of the Supreme Being which ran: 'Quelques femmelettes ont fait des propos inciviques' (Some little women made uncivic remarks) might refer to several dozens of screaming women telling an official exactly what to do with the new deity. The allegation that in a small village of no more than two hundred inhabitants an official ceded the keys of the church in 1796 to several hundreds of fanatical women who threw him to the ground and tore his clothes might mean that the weary official was tired of standing his ground against reiterated insults and petitioning but needed to convince his superiors that he had ceded to *force majeure*. To cite a mere dozen might reveal him for a coward. Or, he might employ a series of euphemisms to cloak the truth. We need to have recourse to specific examples. 'La religion a semé la division dans les familles' (Religion has sown division in families) might be one way of saying that the men are loyal to the religious policy of the Republic but the women are not. What does one make of the Jacobin official who in the post-thermidor months found it needful to comment on the loyalty of his colleagues in the following way: 'il est bon patriot quoi qu'il envoie sa femme à la messe' (He is an excellent patriot although he *sends* his wife to mass)? Does this means that the man had to seem to control his family if he was to hold an official position or does it mean that the Jacobin mayor had despaired of finding anyone whose wife did not go to mass to fill an official position?[7]

We also have to account for the evident scorn of officialdom in the heady days of the Jacobin dictatorship for what they interpreted as women's practices. When, in the year II, it was part of national policy to explain through the national agents *les bienfaits de la Révolution* to those villages and hamlets clearly less than 50 per cent committed to national policies, the rhetoric of persuasion stressed the following: first, that the Revolution represented a victory over political tyranny; second, that it achieved the equality of men; third, that it established the freedom of the individual; and fourth, that it secured the triumph of reason over 'fanatisme.' In this discourse, a model *homme/patriot, femme/fidèle aux prêtres* was allowed to surface. Officialdom clung to the notion that men would embrace the Revolution and that, in the natural order of things, women would in due course follow their husbands. It wallowed in an antifeminism which was indubitably latent in all politicians and which fed on the experience of resistance to its policies. It expected men to see the logic of its arguments. Young men must die for its principles; the rest must make personal sacrifices in the shape of money and goods and wage an unremitting war on the partisans of the old order, who were those who could not accept the crystal-clear logic of *civisme*, who did not respect the maximum, who made *propos inciviques,* or who behaved like women and went to church. It was in the course of this discourse that rural France heard perhaps for the first time the words *philosophie* and *raison* and that age-old practices were *superstition, momerie, fanatisme,* that peasants were the dupes of the enemies of the state. The discourse also made abundantly clear that peasants were considered idiots by the central authority but idiots who could be coaxed or bullied into acceptance of the official line, and the biggest idiots of all in their persistent irrationality were peasant women. When dealing with women, officialdom gave vent to its latent antifeminism in a vocabulary of abuse. Virtually unable to call a woman a woman, it used instead derisive derivatives like *femelles, femelettes, bigotes, bêtes, bêtes de laine, moutons, lentilles, légumineuses, fanatiques.*[8] These are merely a few of the more common nouns which were used in this discourse. The adjectives were still more graphic. Woolly-minded and with an intelligence equivalent to that of a farm animal, the peasant was seen as epitomizing ignorance and stupidity. The general questionnaire sent around in January 1794 to all the districts enquired very closely about local reactions to religious change. The rhetorical vocabulary involved transmits the flavour:

Question: Has the sublime movement of the people against superstition encountered obstacles in its development?[9]

Answer: The sublime movement of the people against superstition has met with very considerable obstacles in its development, [no prizes for saying yes]. We do not believe that these are produced by anything more than ancient prejudices which are always very difficult to overcome when one is dealing with the peasant mind because they are a product of ignorance.[10]

This questionnaire was sent out during the early phases of the dechristianizing campaign; within weeks, the peasant mind in official documents was to be presented not merely as ignorant but also as gendered. There was hope for re-educating the men, as far as officialdom was concerned; women were another matter.

Was the division of men and women in this way by officialdom consonant with the realities? Does available evidence show that officialdom based its analysis on hard evidence or deep-rooted antifeminism? In other words, did the discourse create the issue? Can one weed out fact from fantasy?[11]

It is very obvious that the notion of irrational woman has a venerable history. It is as old as Greek medical treatises, was reaffirmed in renaissance thought, and persisted into modern times. The Enlightenment which immersed woman in nature and made her the creation of her reproductive organs was not prepared to put her on the same rational footing as men. Yet did the promotion of a contrast between manly commitment and female hostility to religious change justified by reference to the differential reasoning power of the two itself create a dichotomy of behaviour between the two? In other words, if the hostility of women is assumed in the rhetoric do women seize upon the role allotted to them? Did the origins of what French religious sociologists have called *le dimorphisme sexuel* (the differential attitude to religious practice between the sexes) conspicuous in the nineteenth and twentieth centuries spring from revolutionary discourse?

Michel Vovelle in his recent study *La Révolution contre l'Eglise* (Paris 1989) is prepared to give serious consideration to the notion that officialdom created the model of the superstitious priest who controlled woman in order to further his own ends and that this effort may have created new problems. He stresses that the *représentants en mission* and local patriots, when dealing with communities of a traditionally anticlerical disposition, might use gender difference to make a bid for the minds of men.[12] To reinforce this notion one might add that whenever the overthrow of the Catholic faith was mooted the terms used assumed an explicitly masculine quality. In November 1793, for example the section of Gravilliers proclaimed to the Convention that it had closed its churches, which had served as lairs for filthy beasts who devoured wealth which should have fed young families and introduced desolation and division into the home. 'Leur enceinte à jamais consacré à la vérité, ne retentira plus que de la voix des Républicains qui instruiront leurs frères, que des mâles accents du patriotisme honorant la raison.'[13]

Some specialist studies of dechristianization show that in particular localities – the Seine et Oise provides the most striking instances – women shared with men in iconoclastic orgies. Yet, when they did so, as in Paris, there could often be considerable ambivalence. When, for example, Saint Eustache in the middle of Les Halles was desecrated, two hundred or more women defended the baptismal chapel and their boast at the end of the day was that the altar cloth was still spotless.[14] The presence of *sans-culotte* women at mass was not uncommon and many expressed unfaltering allegiance to a personage known as *la bonne petite mère*, no less than Mary, the suffering mother of God who also lost her son in a good cause. Such devotion, however, could and did coexist with considerable hatred for particular priests and the higher echelons of the ecclesiastical hierarchy.[15]

In the century preceding the Revolution in most rural parishes a near totality of men and women observed, however perfunctorily, their religious obligations. Those who did not do so rarely accounted for more than 5–6 per cent of the parish and in the extreme west (the Vendée, Brittany, the Cotentin), the east (Alsace, Franche Comté and Lorraine), and Flanders, they were virtually non-existent. In a north to centre block (including the Ile de France, the Seine Valley, Champagne and Western Burgundy, the Auvergne and the Limousin) enclaves could be found with a mixed commitment to regular practice and a significant discrepancy *could* (though this was not necessarily the case) exist between the conformity of adult men and women in respect of Lenten confession and Sunday observance. For example, at Mennecy near Gonesse (Seine et Oise) 91 of 198 male householders, 149 of 198 married women, 28 of 66 bachelors over the age of 25, and a totality of widows and spinsters performed their Easter duties. As one moved further south to the Midi marked contrasts between localities occurred. There were pious mountains and impious garrigues, often *frontières de catholicité* (areas maintaining the faith against the onslaught of Protestantism in an earlier era) and villages of the plains and foothills which could be indifferent to religious demands, some of them perhaps former bastions of heresy which had been forced to express some conformity to Catholicism and which only had a very weak commitment.[16]

The Revolution, however, seems at least in a majority of areas to have accentuated the difference in the commitment of men and women to regular religious practice though we need to make allowances for much local variation and in many cases the difference may only have been one of degree. After 1801 and the formal re-establishment of the Roman Catholic church in France, it was clear that there was a considerable difference in the degree of preparedness of both communities and individuals to return to regular religious worship. As the curé of Ars acknowledged, the battle for the minds of men – who had after all lacked religious instruction in youth or belonged to the revolutionary armies – was much harder to win. In the context of the Revolution the phenomenon of female commitment and male rejection became clearly visible though we must acknowledge significant regional variation.

From what point in the Revolution does the phenomenon manifest itself? Is there a point at which one
can see women rather than men contesting the dismantling of an institution which had been a conspicuous point of reference in their lives? It had, after all,
hallowed the great events of life – birth, marriage, and
death – as well as vaunted the virtues of Catholic motherhood.

There is evidence, though it is much more striking
in some areas than others, of women demonstrating
early hostility to 'intruder' priests in 1790–1 (those who
replaced the nonjurors as parish clergy). Where the in-
cumbent in 1789 was popular and where he made a
personal decision not to accept the oath, then his decision could result in riotous incidents when officialdom read out the notification of legislation insisting
that such an oath be taken in front of the parish.[17] At
this stage, the principles involved in the oath of loyalty
to the constitution probably meant very little to the
women of the parish. Some priests held special meetings to explain their decisions to their parishioners. The
theological niceties involved when they rejected the
oath were then spelled out. Particularly pious spinsters
or widows who were often the main support of the
parish priest and also deeply involved in philantropic
work circulated anti-oath pamphlets and in some towns,
such as Strasbourg, actually organized petitions and
processions in protest against the obligatory nature of
the oath. Perhaps more often, however, the devotion
of rural women was to an individual. The spirit of the
congregation at La Madeleine in Bayeux who yelled
out to the priest 'jurez ou ne jurez pas, cela ne nous
fait rien du tout'[18] may be totally representative. Where
the local priest was prepared to take the oath, as ini-

tially about half of them did, then friction was clearly postponed. The nonjuror who found himself ousted from his presbytery used his firm supports, notably widows and spinsters, to participate in an alternative mass either in the parish church at an unseasonal hour or in a convent chapel. Not only did such activity strip the juror of his congregation but it also ensured that babies were not brought to him for baptism and he was not sought to administer the last rites or burial services. These women did not use the juror's confessional and they did not discourage their sons from assaults on his property. Lacking any influence over village education or control of charitable funds, the constitutional priest became a fervent critic of the behaviour of the women of the parish and an active proponent of a harsher line towards nonjurors. It is from this point that we have the first written complaints from juring priests and administrators about fanatical women who were exercising their influence over their husbands or destroying domestic harmony or even leaving their husbands altogether. Very occasionally in these reports the fear of the quasi-sexual power and attraction of the parish priest over women exercised through the confessional surfaces as it had done under the old regime and would again do *ad nauseam* in the second half of the nineteenth century.[19] Such correspondence embodied commentaries on the inherent female attachment to religion. The juring clergy in their frustration fell back on Eve, declared this time to be influenced through a serpent called the nonjuror.

When in the summer of 1792, the nonjurors had to chose between flight or hiding, their parishioners did not necessarily flock back to their parish church to hear the juror. Some sought out a priest in hiding – though how many were able to do so is a matter of considerable speculation. Chanoine Flament identified about four hundred refractory priests performing services in the Orne, three hundred in the Haute Loire, and one hundred or more in the Sarthe throughout the Revolution.[20] Such figures, however, must be impressionistic and how frequently clandestine masses were held cannot even be guessed. Until the autumn of 1793 the juring clergy, their salary well in arrears and their future compromised by the dechristianizing surge emanating from the Paris sections, nonetheless continued to proffer their services.

After the spring of 1794, however, even the availability of a juror's mass was not to be taken for granted. The dechristianizing campaign had silenced the jurors and the marriage of priests and ceremonial burnings of *lettres de prêtrise* had destroyed whatever shred of credibility remained to the church created by the Constituent Assembly. Where a clandestine ceremony occured, it was held in a private house or barn or illicit chapel and depended upon the complicity or ignorance of local officials and the energy of villagers in carrying out an exercise which could put them in danger of arrest. Such masses were celebrated with least risk in villages distant from prying urban officialdom or were held in a particular household by invitation from the individuals who were hiding the priest. Widows and former members of congregations emerged as those most likely to run the risk of priest sheltering.[21]

Along with the disappearance of a regular mass went the silencing of the parish bell, which had not only been the most constant reminder of religious obligation but had also symbolized community solidarity and had warned of common dangers. On Fridays or Saturdays, it had been commonly rung to call the faithful to confession. Now such a spiritual exercise was rarely available and the habit of confession was generally lost. Nor was there any priest to administer the last rites or to offer catechetical instruction.

What is also abundantly documented is the attack on the old religion in the name of reason. Dechristianization began in Paris and was exported by officialdom, in some instances with an intensity befitting a witch hunt, which far exceeded anything sanctioned by the government. Sometimes, initiatives were local and emanated from the *sociétés populaires*. More often, an ambitious local official, anxious to make his reputation as a patriot and buttressed by an enthusiastic *représentant en mission* emanating from Paris, took initiatives. The *armées révolutionnaires* used iconoclasm and signs of rejection of the old religion as a test of revolutionary commitment.

Conscious of the antagonizing effect of the destruction of the traditional faith upon some of the rural communities, the Robespierrist response was to attempt a substitute devotion based on rationality. There followed from June 1794 a series of state cults – Liberty, Reason, the Supreme Being – all of them promoted as the worship of the rational.

It is pertinent at this point to consider the role played by religion in the lives of the rural masses and in particular to examine the attraction of reason as an abstract notion supplanting the belief in the supernatural in a traditional village. Just what, one might reasonably ask, is rational about life? Some are born crippled or blind, some sick; some get good husbands, some end up with a wife beater; some are fertile and some are barren. Rural society lived with the vagaries of the seasons,

..ought, with hailstorms which could devastate
..rop in an hour. It knew and was powerless against
grain weevils or cattle pest. It still knew periodic vis-
itations of epidemics from smallpox to viral pneumonia
which could eliminate young and old. Some women
died in childbirth; some found the exercise almost ef-
fortless. Viewed in this way, life was not rational but
a grisly lottery in which the stakes were especially
weighted against the poor.

To cope with ever imminent, if not inevitable, disaster, Europeans had over the centuries addressed a
supreme if fitful orchestrator though the intercession
of a priest who commanded knowledge of the relevant
rites and practices. Christians also believed that the
deity could be swayed by penitence and supplication
to saints and above all to Mary. Marianism was by the
eighteenth century perhaps strongest amongst women.
Devotion to a woman who had been elected by this
terrible god to bear his son in a stable and who had
lost a son under terrible circumstances, who knew human suffering, and who, most of all, was prepared to
mediate on behalf of suffering women with a male
deity who could be manipulated – like most men –
through his mother was an intrinsic part of the cult for
women. As the Roman Catholic faith progressively became a fortress faith it was driven back into the home
and hence largely into the hands of women. It became
a faith based on the rosary with its ten Hail Marys for
the one Our Father. The rosary was the perfect expression of a fortress faith. It offerred the one means
whereby the simple and illiterate, stripped of a priesthood and the familiar rituals of church ceremony, could
maintain contact with their deity and could do so collectively. The congregation was replaced by the smaller

unit of the family or the work group gathered, perhaps, for a *veillée* (evening get-together for work in a particular house, partly to economize on heat and light and partly for company). In some regions such as the lacemaking areas of the Velay or Lower Normandy, or areas characterized by high seasonal male migration like the Pyrénées or Savoy, or where male sociability patterns focused on the *cabaret* (tavern) these meetings could be entirely female in composition. The recitation of the rosary, for centuries encouraged by churchmen, now gained new significance as the expression of a corporate faith. Many local officials and even the emissaries of the Comité de Salut Public, the *représentants en mission*, knew about but were prepared to turn a blind eye to such practices. 'Let them have their rosaries,' wrote one *représentant* to the Comité de Salut Publique, 'they will eventually weary of the ridiculous practice and will give it up.' Perhaps such tolerance emanated from the uneasy realization that the wives and mothers of patriots were to be counted amongst the bead tellers. Or, the exercise, when merely performed by women, was perceived to carry no threat. In short, and this did not pass unacknowledged by authority, the faith feminized. It also Marianized.[22] The rosary was not the only expression of this Marianization. The Mother of God herself appeared in woods and grottoes tearfully denouncing the work of the Revolution and the assaults on her personage.

Unlike warm and familiar Mary, the official goddesses seemed ice maidens, quite incapable of contributing anything to the business of living or the business of dying. They commanded no hot line to the deity, no proven record in the alleviation of labour pains or the extermination of grain weevils. Frequently personified, if one could be found, by a young girl whose virginity was deemed beyond question, the goddesses were earthbound, a religious travesty, a living testimony to the ridiculousness of a religion based on reason.

The government knew women were not convinced by the changes just as it was aware that women had most energetically opposed intruder priests and had persistently boycotted the constitutional church. It knew too that there existed rites and practices specific to women which were part of a long process of acculturation. During parturition, for example, a Marian girdle was placed on the mother's heaving stomach to help her in her agony. In messidor of the year II, an article appeared in the *Moniteur* which included the following statement: 'Under a good constitution and a pure sky the parturient mother thinks of the constitution and feels no pain.'[23] One wonders how many put this notion to the test. Very clearly, however, the women's world of rituals impenetrable by the merely male caused a disconcerting shudder, or perhaps no more than a transitory sensation of impotence, amongst the politicians.

The central government did try to offer new ceremonies and festivals to fill what it perceived to be a void. These were, however, largely confined to the large towns. Some local authorities were more cognizant of the need to provide an alternative sociability than others. The Société Populaire de Charolles, for example, on 24 pluviose an II commented on the dissatisfaction and riotous behaviour of women in communes where *les autels de fanatisme* had been destroyed. A debate followed which asked the question: why did women behave in this way? Was it because they had a greater taste for mysticism than men? Of course not. What were the realities of Sunday? Old women walked to church and gossiped with other women and shared meals. This last was important for widows. Young girls went along enthusiastically to gape at the boys in a protected environment. On the décadi, in contrast, men went to the tavern which could never be a suitable place for women and consequently they were left grumbling at home. One solution proposed to win over the women was a dance every décadi which could be chaperoned by the old. This would provide women with an acceptable alternative social outlet and hence render the old religious practices redundant.[24]

Such debates, however, did not solve the immediate problem of what was often a source of bitter contention between women in the parishes and officialdom, the issue of the closure of the church. The government and local officials, perhaps in default of alternative strategies, chose the immediate tactic of appealing to the men and hence attempting to isolate the women from them. Then, and perhaps more persistently from the mid-nineties, it also tried a policy designed to remould the acculturation of the French citizen.

Yet, in spite of knowing and becoming increasingly aware of women's resentment at the destruction of a conventional religion, in the year III when officialdom called upon men to stand up and be counted through oaths of loyalty and *certificates de civisme*, it made no such demands of women. It held that theirs was the private sphere and it was their husbands' job to exercise control. They were not citizens that is those partaking of the political, but citizenesses, owing first allegiance to the responsible citizen in the shape of husband or father. Their relationship to politics placed them at one remove. Let the citizen bring them to obedience.

Some clubs and *sociétés populaires* encouraged men to force their wives into gestures of contempt for the Catholic faith. For such efforts the officials were subsequently to pay dearly. The insistence of the *société populaire* at Arles, for example, that every male householder bring his wife to a ceremony where they could spit in unison upon the host to show that he was a patriot husband in control of his household may help to explain why these officials were so brutally murdered during the White Terror.[25] Certainly, the attitude of the central government was that male obedience was the priority and that the obedience of irrational woman was of less significance. A woman's acts were in the first instance to be regulated by her husband. This existence at one remove from state control may have opened up some scope for subversive activity: the actions of women were to a degree condoned. This should not, however, be taken too far. Women died on the scaffold for their beliefs, if not as often as did men, and there is nothing, as Olympe de Gouges pointed out, apolitical about the guillotine.

The Terror not only demanded an appraisal of how one felt about the Revolution but also, by a new intrusiveness, applied the letter of revolutionary law with a new determination. It came forward with a new brand of officialdom prepared to push the law in some instances far beyond the intention of the Comité de salut public and this officialdom dominated departmental and local authorities and the *sociétés populaires*. This officialdom defined itself as the agent of reason, the disciple of philosophy. It took upon itself the function of converting the people, if need be through force and confrontation. It is from the pens of this officialdom that our version of counter-revolutionary woman emerges. It is not a neutral source, for this macho culture dreaded loss of face and sought scapegoats for its failures.[26] Nevertheless, it did not invent counter-revolutionary women and though we need to be hypercritical of the evidence, it cannot be ignored.

The examples which will now be used are proffered to re-create the figure of the counter-revolutionary woman from the Haute Loire.[27] We are fortunate to be able to draw on the maps of Michel Vovelle and Timothy Tacket to follow the ripples of the dechristianizing movement. The Haute Loire was not as tranquil as the Aube or the Pas de Calais but nor was it as immediately oppositional as the Vendée, Franche Comté, or the Lyonnais. It did not come out in open revolt like its neighbour, the Gévaudan and it worried the government less than did the contiguous Puy de Dome. It is an area of impenetrable gorges, crags, with mountain streams and inadequately roads. It is not an easy place to penetrate and one might have thought it possible to live out one's life there relatively untroubled by the Revolution. Terror, after all, was without doubt at its most successful on flat land where communications were good and news of insubordination travelled easily.[28] However, the area was to experience a group of ambitious local officials, the home-brewed equivalent of Maximilien de Robespierre, headed by Solon Reynaud, an ex-priest, one time mayor of Le Puy (1789), later in control of the department and Paris deputy, who chose to try to make his reputation in the area. He spoke of himself as the Couthon of the Haute Loire and hence was to confront the practices of the past in a particularly nasty and authoritarian manner. The department boasted the greatest number of guillotined priests in France. Moreover this was a region whose

economy suffered particularly in the context of Revolution. It was a lacemaking economy directed and
worked by women. These two factors allow us perhaps
to paint a counter-revolutionary woman in very vivid
oils rather than more delicate pastels. La Ponote and
the woman of the Velay may not be totally typical but
nor are they totally abnormal. There is no single model,
perhaps, of counter-revolutionary woman but there are
variations on a number of basic themes.

In this area, then, our counter-revolutionary woman
was a lacemaker out of work because of the slump in
luxury commodities. She lived in a hamlet, rather than
a nuclear village. She had received her education at
the hands of a *béate*, a local widow or spinster who
lived in a house owned by the village in exchange for
teaching girls to make lace and to recite the catechism
and who in the evening organized work sessions in
which lighting and heating were shared. The bell above
her door punctuated the phases of the day and in winter when the snow fell and the church was unreach-
able, the *béate* replaced the priest and read a holy story
and organized hymn singing.[29] When the Catholic
church became a schismatic church, she clung to the
nonjuror and her premises became the locale of the
clandestine church. In this way, though with progres-
sive disenchantment both economically and socially,
the villages of the Velay weathered the first three years
of Revolution. The status quo, however, was to be dramatically challenged by the advent in the summer of
1793 of the conventionnel Reynaud who had political
ambitions and wished to make his name at a national
level. He identified religion as the disintegrant and dis-
affective factor in the relationship between the state
and its citizenry. He took it upon himself, aided by a

team of subordinates, to make war on a religion of royalism and women, the latter graphically described by him as *cette vermine malfaisante*.[30] His attack had a specific gender approach and it produced a specific gender response. His tactics could be thus summarized: first a more overt attack on the juring priesthood backed by the erection of a permanent guillotine at Le Puy; second, an attack on *les signes extérieures du culte*, bells, statues, crucifixes worn around the necks of women; third, the institution of the décadi, civil marriage and burial and penalties for non-observance. A particular eye was to be kept on women here because they were prone to ignore the décadi and he suggested some token arrests. The heaviest punitive action was of course against the priest. Lastly an end was to be put to the *béate* and her activities. She must be forced to take a civil oath in front of the women of the village or small town. This was in fact overstretching the law.

It was in response to this package that counter-revolutionary woman learned her techniques. The first was collective obstinacy – there was no room in this situation for individual heroism because an insurgent individual could be easily picked off whilst the women of an entire village acting together were much less vulnerable. The second technique was to use ridicule of an explicitly sexual or sexist variety. The spirit of such ridicule was in the vein of 'imagine grown men taking all this trouble with little us and see how we can embarrass you.' The third was to isolate an official recognized as weak or isolated in his devotion to the central line. The fourth was to vote with one's feet on issues where maternal authority mattered. These techniques, presently to be exemplified, were learned during the Terror and perfected under the Directory whose intent was to give the Revolution a second chance and this policy was to necessitate a second, if much emasculated, terror. This terror was in turn undermined by a war of attrition, much of it the work of women.

The first example of action by women is chosen to demonstrate the efficacy of standing one's ground in opposition to a particular issue and seeing how far obstinacy could go. We are in Montpigié, a small town with three sections in ventôse an III (February 1795) and Albitte, one of the *représentants en mission* boasting the most success as a dechristianizer, has arrived from Le Puy to receive the oath of loyalty from the *béates*. He has decided to make a holiday of the event and announces that the women of each section should gather separately in the Temple of Reason because it is important that the women should see their leader being brought into line: 'We summoned girls and women, female patriots, female aristocrats, the stupid, the *béates* [a play on the words *bêtes* and *béates*] without distinction to assemble in their section. I did not count on the fanatical hotheads presenting themselves. I was, overjoyed to see a large assembly of stupid little women.

He took to the tribune and addressed them in terms designed to be understandable to the mentally retarded: 'I outlined the simplicity, the necessity and the importance of the oath they were asked to take: the bloody horrors of fanaticism and the belief of republicans in the existence of a gracious god who can only be worshipped by the practice of virtue and not by an exterior cult, full of theatricality and all for nothing.'[31]

He then asked for the handful of *béates* from Montpigié and the surrounding hamlets to take the oath. They stood up and announced themselves prepared to go to the guillotine rather than express loyalty to a

pagan regime. Immediately all the other women present got to their feet and cheered resoundingly. These
women, Albitte protested, were mothers of families and
acting contrary to their husbands' wishes, the latter
being absent. Seeing this, he said, he had no option
but to dismiss the assembly and try again. The next
day he had got a few guards to support him and tried
another section of the town. This time, before he had
had time to enter the tribune, a *béate* touched him on
the arm and said she was ready for the guillotine now.
The women of the village came to her support. Albitte's
men moved in and rounded up about a hundred although the town did not have a really safe prison and
this proved a considerable error. By evening the husbands of the married women facing household chores
and coping with their children were demanding the
release of their wives. The mayor's refusal to comply
led to a gaol rising a few days later with a concerted
effort from within and without. The *représentant en
mission* released the married women and sent them
home. They promptly mobilized the other women of
the town. There was then a concentrated attack on the
prison which resulted in the liberation of the *béates* and
the incarceration of the mayor and the national agent.

It will be immediately apparent that no regime can
support this kind of loss of face. At the same time, to
move in the National Guard with its relatively heavy
weaponry to confront rebellious but unarmed womanhood was not the answer to the problem. There were
armed confrontations between guards and women with
some loss of life on both sides but the guards were
demeaned by such confrontation and not all were convinced of the need for an oath or by the dechristianizing
campaign. Moreover, many of the protesting women

were mothers or grandmothers who exercised their own kind of authority over the young guard and often used their first names. Authority was safest when it could pick off offenders one by one. Then there was less risk of loss of official dignity.

The most humiliating scenes for authority were without any doubt enacted less during the dechristianizing campaign than when authority sought to promote alternative deities – Reason, Liberty, the Supreme Being, who followed in quick succession in 1794. All of them were major disasters. One of the most graphic incidents occurred at Saint Vincent near Lavoûte sur Loire, former seat of the Polignacs and a place far from committed to the old regime or to the Revolution. The occasion was an instruction from Le Puy to read, on the décadi, in the Temple of Reason, a paean to the Supreme Being (June 1794). In the front row sat the local dignitaries, their wives and children. The unlucky celebrant began his patriotic oration when, at a sign from an old woman, the entire female audience rose, turned their backs on the altar of liberty, and raised their skirts to expose their bare buttocks and to express their feelings to the new deity. Confronted by the spectacle of serried rows of naked female backsides the celebrant was reduced to gibberish. Officialdom departed in unseemly haste with aspersions on its manhood made from all sides. The humiliated celebrant wrote in anger to the department about his impotence before *ces gestes gigantesques et obscènes*.[32] News of this incident promoted its replication in the nearby bourgs of Lavoûte and across the hills at Saint Paulhien. '*Montrer le cul aux gens* as an expression of female scorn has a long history in France even before Zola enshrined the practice in *Germinal*. It was emphatically a tech-

nique of the working classes. The middle-class or re-
fined equivalent was simply to turn one's back or to
sit on one's heels.

In two areas women could sabotage official policy
and ideology virtually without effort. The control of
birth and death were in the hands of women. The first
was contained within the home; anyone could slap a
cross on an infant brow. More disconcerting because it
spilled over into the public domain was the preparation
for death and the burial of the defunct.

Most people are attended in their final suffering by
women. Hence, in the present context, their exit was
in the hands of those likely to summon a clandestine
priest or a female ex religious. The last could not pronounce absolution but she could urge the dying to re-
pentence and reassure his or her relatives that they had
fulfilled their spiritual obligations and opened up the
gates of paradise. The juring clergy had from 1791 faced
a rejection of their services to the dead and humiliating
incidents such as the leaving of the corpses of rotting
animals in the parish church for burial. Such gestures
stripped the jurors of their hold over the populace. A
priest who did not have the keys to the kingdom of
heaven could not be taken seriously. Yet to obtain a
Christian burial from a nonjuring priest was progressively difficult after 1793 and so in the Haute Loire
groups of women undertook the burial, if need be at
the dead of night. There is, of course, good biblical
precedent for the laying away of the dead by faithful
women. The contests which could emerge over the issue of burial constitute my third illustrative tale.

The incidents occurred in Canton Vert, the revolutionary name for what had been and is now Chaise
Dieu.[33] It is found in a series of letters written by the

municipal agent in the year VI. The letters, however, relate to incidents stretching back over a longer period. The Directory was committed to freedom of worship provided the celebrant took an oath. To take such an oath of loyalty to the Republic or indeed any oath required by the government exposed any priest to rejection by the community. As in this case, the community might attempt to run an alternative church using a clandestine priest or someone who knew the liturgy.

The municipal agent of Canton Vert was also a constitutional priest who had suffered imprisonment for failing to surrender his *lettres de prêtrise* (the documents bestowing priesthood upon him). After the laws of ventôse an III (February, 1795) he struggled to re-establish parochial worship only to find himself frustrated by the women of the bourg who found an effective leadership in a Sister of Saint Joseph du Puy who ran a counter church, organized clandestine masses, and served as the agent for a hidden nonjuror. Worse, she did all this from a house right opposite the legally acceptable church presided over by the agent-priest.

His letters of protest to the department described body snatching. He recounted how one Sister of Saint Joseph could gather together at any time about thirty fanatical women (*fanatiques*) to help her but that she assumed the role of director, orchestrating the event. The women would surround the body and when the relatives tried to intervene and insist that it should go to the church where the priest had taken an oath of loyalty, the thirty or more 'furies and harridans' would attack the relatives and drive them away by throwing stones. In the particular instance that the agent proceeded to recount in some detail, the relatives were only ten in number and were totally intimidated and retired leaving the disposal of the body to the women. Next day there was an open clash on the issue between the priest and the Sister of Saint Joseph. The slanging match is worth recounting since it was done publicly and the priest/agent was humiliated. He called her a *fanatique, druide, mégère, énergumène* (a fanatic, a druid, a vixen, and a fury). She called him a *secteur de Calvin, philosophe*, a disciple of the devil and its child the Republic.[34] Her insults were lent force by a large crucifix which she was carrying when the altercation occurred and she advanced towards him waving it as if to exorcize the devil. As a *signe extérieure du culte*, the crucifix was quite illegal but it helped her to win the contest game, set, and match and she was cheered on by the onlookers. The curé appealed to the department: 'Rid us of these counter-revolutionary tricksters ... The Sister of Saint Joseph du Puy as the chief of the fanatics should be pursued with all possible publicity [*avec éclat*] in order to deter the rest. Have the high priestess removed and overthrow her temple and her altar and place a prohibition on their re-establishment with a penalty for infraction ... Frightened by the example made of their abbess, the other women will return to their duty.'[35]

Rentrer dans le devoir was exactly the consummation authority devoutly wished as its woman policy. To get the female population back into the home and obedient to husband and the law was summed up in this simple phrase.

The thermidoreans, confronted with the problems emanating from dearth and the general weariness of local officialdom after 1795 in face of the penury of funds and the hostility of the rural populaces, were prepared to concede a great deal. The law of ventose year III (21 February1795) granted freedom of worship but precluded communes acquiring as a collectivity a church for community worship. It did not cede the parish church although it left to local authorities the option on offering such a building by auction. However, only individuals were allowed to bid and such individuals were then responsible before the law for what occurred within its walls. Resolutely, all exterior manifestations of religious affiliation were prohibited. There were to be no bells, no processions, no banners, no pilgrimages. If the Christian religion was celebrated within the church or elsewhere, only clergy who had taken a civil oath of loyalty might officiate. In short, and whilst explicitly committing itself to the official cults, the thermidoreans ceded something but it fell far short of what many communities wanted.

The policies of the thermidoreans were interpreted at the local level in very different ways. Some who took office in the aftermath of the Terror had overtly 'royalist,' that is to say anti-Jacobin, tendencies and were prepared to turn a blind eye to what was going on. Others adopted a much harder line.[36] The government's decision to let Catholic worship occur provided it was contained within the framework outlined above was doomed to failure because by mid-1795 a religious revival was underway and in many, if not all regions, this revival was female orchestrated. The west, where religion fuelled civil war, and the east, where exiled clergy could return more easily and assume direction, provide strong exceptions to the more general picture. The pattern of the religious revival and the emotions which fuelled it varied between individuals and social groups, between villages, between town and country, and between one geographical location and another. It depended too upon how local officials were prepared to ignore much of what was happening. In some areas, the anarchy of the period allowed religion to resurface relatively unchecked. For women in large towns and cities, particularly in the Paris provisioning zone which formed a two-hundred-mile radius around the city and included cities like Rouen and Amiens, dearth prompted a desperate search for religious solace. Even in Paris, a police official commented on two queues, one at the baker's and one for mass.[37]

For many urban women, there was more than a touch of guilt for a political past in which they had been very active collaborators, and the return to religion was by way of atonement. No such sense of personal guilt tinged the attitudes of rural women. In their view, what had happened was the fault of others. If the thermidoreans had hoped that their tolerance would bring peace, they were to be disillusioned.

To reconstruct the devotional patterns of the past, communities needed to take a number of basic steps. These were: the restoration of the church to its primitive usage; the procuring of sacred vessels and the means to summon the faithful to mass; the restitution of Sunday and the rejection of the décadi as the day of rest and the one on which an individual could fulfil his or her obligations and participate in a community ceremony. Then, at some stage, the decision had to be made of whom should be asked to officiate at the parish mass but this was seen as a secondary to securing the ancient locale for public worship.

Where local officialdom was prepared to hire out the church at auction and where such auctions have been carefully studied, as have those in Normandy by the Abbé Sévestre, then women, particularly widows, are seen to have been in the forefront.[38] Even at impious Gonesse where some women had participated in the dechristianizing surge, 'les femmes menaient l'action.' At Mende, there was a curious contest for the honour of restoring the cathedral as parish church. Two women were rival contenders. One, Rose Bros, wife of a tailor and leader of a bread riot in 1789, proffered three hundred livres. Given the penury of her circumstances, it seems unlikely that the money was hers but rather that she was known as a courageous activist and was prepared to take the lead. Another woman, however, made a rival bid. She was Citoyenne Randon, wife of a former district official during the Terror. Her actions raise a string of questions. Was she distancing herself from her husband's past record? Was she seeking to save his skin from the fury of the populace in changing times? Was she anxious to wrench control from a troublemaker believing that she could direct the developing situation better?[39] Did the women (largely, it would appear, widows with some means) generally act on their own behalf or on that of the community as a whole believing that the work of women would be shrugged off if reported to a timid set of officials? There are occasional instances of husbands denouncing the activities of their wives but others may have been pleased enough to shelter behind their activities. However, what is clear is that in matters of religion in many of the villages and bourgs of provincial France, women dominated the public action. They did not sit obediently at home.

If no auctions were held, then very frequently riots occurred in which the doors of the church were forced and the community simply occupied the building, cleaned it up, and made it available for worship. News

of a successful occupation in one community often encouraged surrounding ones to make a similar attempt.
The riots had a distinctive form characteristic of female
protest movements. The weaponry did not exceed stones
and ashes. Women relied on their special status as
women to promote their cause. Old and pregnant
women were placed in the forefront and the rest, frequently bolstered by women from neighbouring parishes, brought up the rear with their aprons full of ashes
to throw in the eyes of any opposition.[40] If they succeeded in laying hold of the church, then they might
move on to confront the official whom they thought
to be guardian of religious vessels, or entire communities might rally to achieve the pealing of the bells.
This act was the one encountering the most stubborn
opposition from officialdom since a pealing bell pronounced to the outside world that republican law was
ignored in the community.[41] It pointed to their failure
to control the situation in their parish, and it is the
issue of the bells that provokes the most exaggerated
accounts of women confronting unwilling officialdom.
Often the seizure of the bell, followed by its rebellious
peal, was used to symbolize local triumph over official
policy and the angelus was tolled up to three times a
day. In towns and larger villages, however, particularly
those which were accessible, such activities brought out
the National Guard and officials forced a more discreet
religion upon the people. At Montpellier failure to gain
control of the bells meant that those anxious to gather
for parish worship had to fall back on the cowbell rung
by small boys sent into the streets by their mothers.[42]

Other issues were in their way decisive but took the
citadel of republican authority by sap rather than direct
confrontation. Amongst such issues was that of Sunday

versus the décadi, the tenth day of rest decreed by the Jacobins when a republican calendar was inaugurated. Resented at the popular level as an evident reduction of leisure, to rural women, since the event was accompanied by no ritual or extended social contact, the laicized feast seemed a sham. The populace voted on this issue with its feet but the lead was frequently given by women giving their servants Sunday, not the décadi, as partial holiday.

Time off for the working man during the early nineties had come to mean drinking and for many men tavern sociability was a more than acceptable alternative to religious ritual. Under the ancien régime, this was a choice denied to many since the opening hours of the *cabaret* were limited on Sundays and *fêtes*. However, the removal of the curé as a check on the tavern keeper's business led to a burgeoning of tavern sociability. Associated also with local politics as the meeting place of the *société populaire*, the tavern became a more widely used place by men but not one for respectable women.[43]

Frequently Sunday was hallowed by men lounging in the tavern whilst the women went to mass but the very indolence of the men on the sabbath was itself interpreted as an act of protest.[44] Certainly, and this was particularly apparent in the years immediately after the Concordat before the church had mobilized itself anew to make a bid for the allegiance of men, the return of women to regular religious worship was far more conspicuous than was that of their menfolk.

It was very important that the renascent church should be served by personnel acceptable to the women. Where possible, this meant a nonjuror but such a personage could only operate illegally and hence much depended upon the compliance of the local authorities in turning a blind eye to his activities. Where a nonjuror could not be found, or where local circumstances were hostile to such illegal activity, women contented themselves with the services of a lay figure who knew the liturgy. Such a person could not offer communion but he satisfied the local need for a ceremony which was an expression of community solidarity. This practice disquieted churchmen and hostile lay authorities alike but it was well within the letter of the law.

The rejection of the juror by women caused the Abbé Grégoire extreme bitterness; his efforts to seize the initiative for the constitutional church in re-establishing Catholic worship were frustrated by what he termed *des femmes crapuleuses et séditieuses*.[45]

Perhaps, however, the *messes blanches*, or 'blind masses' as they were called, tell us a great deal about what women valorized in religion. They rejoiced in a safe expression of community sociability, the warmth and comfort of a religion with visible rituals, and those *signes extérieurs du culte* which both jurors and nonjurors were at pains to stress were of least spiritual significance to the Catholic faith. They were relatively indifferent to actual clerics themselves. Although there are instances of loyalty to one individual parish priest sustained throughout the Revolution, an uninterrupted relationship was rare. Driven underground and subjected often to considerable physical suffering in order to keep their identities secret from the authorities, many of the emergent nonjuring clergy were in very poor physical shape, and the lack of new recruits increasingly took its toll upon their numbers. This perhaps did not matter if rituals could be replicated. Their absence was then not noted.

The returning clerics wanted penitence. In the immediate context of famine, they got it but progressively after 1798 this spirit faltered. City women and men fell away and though the rural congregations remained large, the peasants did not expect to make financial sacrifices for their deity. The returning clergy claimed that interest in catechism classes and sending for the priest to perform the last rites were lost habits which no one was interested in reacquiring. They feared that they had lost control of the minds of an entire generation which had grown up without formal religious instruction other than that which the family could bestow.

The religious revival of the late 1790s occurred against a background of resolute opposition in the localities to government policies. If women's protest focused on re-establishing a church, that of young men took the form of draft dodging and desertion. By 1795, volunteers and conscripts no longer deserted in ones or twos but en masse, taking with them their weapons and effects. We hear of whole companies of soldiers in full uniform – which became progressively more bedraggled as the days wore on – walking the roads of France. One group crossed a half-dozen departments without being challenged.[46] In order to survive, such gangs robbed the countryside mercilessly. Whilst some returned home, others lived in woods and mountainous areas known to their relatives, who helped to keep them provisioned. We hear most reports of desertion from the departments of the Massif Central, the Alps, and the Pyrénées and of course from the Vendée. There was no longer any emotive appeal to arms in defence of the Republic. The politicians tried to blame the English and 'emissaries of royalism.' Lacking the repressive forces necessary to round up the young men and fearful of the consequences of making desertion a capital offence lest still more defections occurred, authority lost control of the situation. Occasionally, it tried to stage a show trial as in the round-up of Jehu and his companions in the Haute Loire in 1798. This band, allegedly of several hundred young men, had gained an evil reputation for uncontrolled brigandage. To bring them to justice once captured, the Directory sanctioned a cordon around Le Puy lest a prison break should be attempted. Jehu, however, like Macheath in Gay's opera, won the heart of the prison warder's daughter who managed to get him out of jail, and the forces of authority suffered conspicuous loss of face. Other young men sought to get out of their military commitment by severing the fingers on their right hand so that they could not fire a rifle. In the Tarn the suggestion was made to dress such cowards in women's bonnets and march them round the town on the décadi, so that this parade might have the effect of drawing to the revolutionary spectacle 'a public utterly indifferent to republican institutions.'[47] Cobb and Forrest are insistent that desertion was one of the most effective means the common people had of expressing their hostility to a regime which had repressed and impoverished them and to which they felt no commitment.[48]

For older men, those who did not have to go to war, there was a dangerous form of passive resistance which took the form of not paying taxes, idling in the tavern on a Sunday, and working in flagrant disrespect on the décadi. There was, however, in the Midi, a deadlier form of revenge on former terrorist supporters. Deserters played their part in flushing out republican strongholds but there was also a communal violence in which the adult males of a village or small town formed a gang of *égorgeurs* (throat slitters), who did not in fact do what their name suggested but beat up or threatened, insulted and humiliated, the households of men who were identified as former Jacobins, the supporters of Terror. Such violence was not the work of women but the latter could provide the incitement for action and contribute to the atmosphere of hostility by extending threats to the wives and children of those identified with Jacobin government.[49] In part, we may be looking at a kind of squaring of the record in societies where the vendetta flourished and without this act of revenge for loved ones lost or families severed by the revolutionary record, normality could not be achieved.

However, such an interpretation must not obscure the violence or the anarchy of this period. The more one familiarizes oneself with the years 1796–1801, the more apparent it becomes that the attempt by women to establish a pattern of religious worship, and an expression of community solidarity which simultaneously hallowed the structure of family life, was the most constructive force one can determine at work in society. It was one which was working in the direction of normalization and a return to a structured lifestyle. Peacefully but purposefully, they sought to re-establish a pattern of life punctuated by a pealing bell and one in which rites of passage – birth, marriage, and death – were respected and hallowed. The state had intruded too far and women entered the public arena to push it back and won. It was one of the most resounding political statements to be made by the populace in the entire history of the Revolution.

CHAPTER FOUR

Epilogue. The Legacy: Myth and Memory

Epilogue. The Legacy: Myth and Memory

Eugenie: Un moment Caroline. Etes-vous aristocrate ou démocrate?
Caroline: Je suis femme de chambre.

Madame de la Charrière, *Oeuvres Complètes*
(Geneva, 1797, vol. 7, 418)

The years between 1795 and 1798 offered no consolation to those who had made a significant emotional investment in the Revolution. The administrators upon whom the Directory depended at the local level were committed to an uphill and in the long run futile effort to preserve what they believed to be worth saving in the Revolution.[1] Not only had they to try to govern the localities without a viable currency and were they themselves without personal remuneration but they had to contend with a disillusioned, cynical, and frankly hostile populace, one that realized that the promises of politicians and their grandiloquent rhetoric were devoid of meaning.

There were few who were not weary of demands for personal sacrifice and as many who felt themselves duped. They had been encouraged to believe in *les bienfaits de la Révolution* and the evils of aristocracy but in face of food shortages and demands for military resources in the form of money and men, the populace ceased to listen to the politicians in whatever guise they came. Caroline, and she carried with her in her sentiments the entire working populace, in Belle de la Charrière's pungent phrase, willingly depoliticized herself. She was neither aristocrat nor democrat but a chambermaid. As such, she had only her own personal survival to bear in mind.

The thermidoreans and the Directory had few police and only limited soldiers at their disposal to help contain the anarchy that pervaded provincial France. Added to this, the thermidoreans, though their embittered successors perhaps less so, believed, and often quite sincerely, that the Terror was the reason for the loss of popular support for the Revolution in much of rural France. They hoped, against the odds, that the dismantling of the institutions of the Terror and the emasculation of former officials who had been responsible for an overzealous commitment to the Terror would in themselves help to reconcile to the current political status quo those overtly hostile to the Revolution.

Nonante cinq, as 1795 was referred to in popular lore, was dubbed by Richard Cobb as the year of the loss of illusions.[2] By this he meant that there was an official abandonment of the pretence that government policies had been sound or had worked but for the opposition of a dissident minority. Colin Jones called it the year of the U-turns.[3] Policies to which there had been an apparently total and explicit commitment since 1790, such as the right of the poor – specifically defined – to state assistance, were dropped without any real dissent. The politicians opted, at least temporarily, for religious tolerance: they opened the prison doors and they stopped pretending that the state could succour the poor and extolled the virtues of *bienfaisance individuelle*.

Individuals emerged in the bosom of the rump Convention who facilitated these reversals in attitude. Delacloy, for example, an individual whose political record was far from distinguished, permitted the exit from state commitment to subsidies (which admittedly were months if not years in arrears) to the patriotic poor and eased the return to private charity.[4] It was as if the Comité de Mendicité and indeed the enlightenment writings on poverty had never existed. Overnight, public state-based assistance, not private charity, was blamed for unrealistic claims on the public purse.

Others, as we have seen, urged the need to substitute religious tolerance for persecution, provided of course that certain rules were respected. Perhaps the only positively consistent policies the thermidoreans consciously strove to promote were an explicit commitment to the rule of law in the face of burgeoning anarchy and a belief in state education which it was hoped would eventually educate the masses in the ways of republicanism.

Even those limited objectives were doomed to failure. The politicians could not stem the tide of the religious revival and they could not get the populace into the state schools. They could not stop the White Terror, a

war of revenge against former revolutionary patriots
which erupted in the Midi, and they certainly could
not stem the flow of deserters from military service.
They could not even get the taxes in. In 1795–6 less
than 9 per cent of the national budget was realized.
They tried a reversion to terror but lacked the means
in terms of forces of repression and the commitment
to sustain it. They merely created a new group of martyrs.

The Napoleonic coup d'état of 1799 simply set the
seal on what many republicans recognized as the defeat
of their ideals. Infinitely weary and infinitely embittered, they brooded on the reasons for their failure.

Amongst the first truly sincere and committed republicans who struggled to explain to himself what had
gone wrong was Portal, national agent in the Haute
Loire who had laboured sincerely to reconcile to the
Revolution a region which had been bitterly alienated.
Initially he had blamed the conventionnel Solon Reynaud for a tactless handling of the situation. Overzealous and overambitious Reynaud, he stated with
more than a touch of bitterness, had exceeded his brief
in order to enhance his own reputation. Portal extolled
firmness in moderation and the need to take a long-
term view. Given the centuries of ignorance in which
the populace had been locked, he tried to persuade
himself that time and the inherent logic of the republican belief in reason and the sovereignty and centrality
of the state which was dedicated to the well-being of
its citizenry must ultimately permit republicanism to
triumph. As a former priest, he was prepared to feel
tolerant of those who clung to the Christian faith but
he insisted firmly on the need for an oath of loyalty
from officiating clerics and put a great deal of energy

into the creation of state schools with state salaried teachers. He strenuously eschewed violence, deeming the prevention of martyrs essential to the promotion of republicanism. Within two years, however, open flouting of the legislation, particularly that relative to the refusal of returning nonjuring clergy to take an oath of loyalty, caused him to deal progressively in verbal threats and token house searches.

For Portal, and those like him, republicanism meant an overriding commitment to the state and to the rule of law. The state was the guarantor of essential liberties; it was egalitarian in that it turned its back on aristocracy and privilege; it was tolerant but insistent that it must command the first loyalty of its citizens. It was also rational in so far as it denied arbitrariness and allegiance to any divinely imposed moral code. It endorsed many of the moral standards of the Christian religion but divorced them from a religious justification. After four years of struggle, Portal asked himself why republicanism and his efforts to promote it had encountered such a resounding failure.

His answer was prophetic. he attributed his defeat to a slip of a girl, *une fille sachant lire*. He called her an independent woman, a *béguine*, a *béate*. This woman was prepared to educate children for nothing. She offered a package which included *les rêveries du papisme* and made the children under her tutelage *abjurer tout sentiment de raison*. She prepared the children to take communion and hallowed the priest who officiated. Still more dangerous, she controlled the minds of the next generation through their mothers. Worst of all, she 'painted the Republic as the work of the devil.'5

Portal's *fille* in the Haute Loire was a *béate*, the lacemaker schoolmistress who gave her services freely to the community in exchange for her keep. Portal saw her as the linchpin in a complex relationship between priest and people which served to exclude the rational politician and undermine his influence. Along with other national agents, disillusioned Jacobins and more moderate republicans, Portal laid the foundations of an important tradition in the republican interpretation of the Revolution, that is that the whole event was undermined by irrational woman who was the ignorant support of papistry. Long before there was any push to demand political rights for women in the second half of the nineteenth century the equation of women with the triumph of clericalism was written in stone.

This interpretation of why republicanism failed emerged very explicitly in the 1840s when Michelet, who was to become the most powerful exponent of the threat women constituted to political progress, published *Le Prêtre, la femme et la famille* (Paris 1845), an extraordinarily influential work which was reprinted eight times before 1875. A decade later he produced *La Femme et la Révolution française* (Paris 1854). These works reveal a somewhat different emphasis. In the first, the confessional is interpreted as the means whereby the church controlled women and converted them into a power base. The priest intruded into the running of the family and hence usurped the power of the husband/patriarch. The husband's views were contradicted and undermined by a spiritual tyrant who held his wife in fear. Michelet pressed in this work for the elimination of this intruder in family unity. In Rousseau's vein he extolled the companionate marriage wherein the rational male kindly directed his spouse without tyrannical intrusion. *Let the religion of the home replace religion.* Content with kindness and at one with her husband, the wife and mother could rear her children in harmony with her mate. The Sophie paradigm surfaced.

In the second work, however, woman appears not as the tool of the priest but vice versa. Michelet's close examination of the evidence of the Vendée, wherein he drew upon oral testimony, suggested to him that women, because of a surfeit of sensibility, could not rest easy with the destruction of church power and they therefore became intrepid defenders of the faith. Through remorseless seditious activity, mainly in the bedroom, they restored the priest to the parish. Michelet was perhaps seeking to explain why, when the priest was removed from the parish, and hence could not exert pressure through the confessional, he was not obliterated from the political spectrum. Michelet felt obliged, however, to acknowledge that women were capable of considerable initiatives. He lauded their activities in October 1789 but thereafter saw them as pernicious and guileful though their intentions may have been pure. It was in the home that men were undermined and deflected from rational action because they ceded to the sensibility of women. The authority of men, and by extension that of the state, was thus sapped. It followed in this rendering that women were made powerful through domestic influence and that unless such power could be controlled by the state then republicanism was doomed to eternal failure.

Michelet's switch in emphasis may have reflected the passing of his mistress. He was excluded from her deathbed by confessor, doctor, and family. He believed that she was the victim of the insidious priesthood empowered through the confessional. His work became a foundation text for denouncing the threat to family morality posed by an outside intruder.[6] However, the reversals of republicanism after the revolutions of 1848 and Michelet's own studies of the Revolution, the evidence he consulted, and the women to whom he spoke pushed him to endow woman with greater powers – a change in emphasis not popular amongst his intellectual peers. The French intelligentsia was prepared to concede that the Catholic church was propped up by gullible women but not that women controlled the priesthood. They wanted to assert that women were orchestrated by a machiavellian clergy responsible for all the initiatives. Women were hence not primarily responsible though that did not make them any the less powerful instruments. For all republicans, and this included Michelet, the real enemy, it should be stressed, was the church which vaunted faith over justice and reason. Women, however, were identified as the death-watch beetles which ate away the underpinning of the rationalist stance in the home. Whether or not they were prime agents of the failure of the first attempt at republicanism mattered less than the process of destruction and the fatal alliance between women and the clergy.

How justified was an interpretation of the events of 1793–1801 which blamed women for the failure of the Revolution? We have seen that women were indeed much more explicit in their defence of Catholicism than were their menfolk; yet to elect religious conflict as the sole reason for the defeat of republicanism was to ignore 90 per cent of the story. Sense not sensibility undermined the Revolution. It could not deliver the economic goods. It foundered in inflation, poor harvests, an expensive war, a currency which no one believed in, and extreme deprivation for too large a proportion of its populace. Describing the descent into brigandage which marked much of western, central, and southern France in 1796, Marcel Marion gave as reasons 'démoralisation générale, mépris de la vie humaine, trop enseigné par les évènements de la Révolution, crise économique intense, misère extrême, perte de l'habitude de travail, profonde division dans la société, timidité et impuissance de la répression.'[7] The summary would seem to suffice to explain the failure of the high hopes of 1789. The Revolution had demanded too much of both men and women.

If we follow the experience of the years 1789–99 from a consumer's viewpoint and think of what it might mean in the lives of ordinary people, then the discredit of the Revolution becomes fully understandable. It is perhaps true that women were 'privileged victims,' as Michelet suggested, in that they were the lowest earners and the most vulnerable when unemployment loomed. If we think of the Revolution from the point of view of the maidservant, the lacemaker, the silk reeler, the embroiderer, or the maker of stays or fans or lingerie of all kinds, or the laundress unable to lay hold of soap in the year II, or the mother of an illegitimate child dependent upon the work of her hands, or the prostitute forced to offer her services in 'nonante cinq' *pour un morceau de pain*, because that was the going rate, then we can appreciate that enthusiasm for the Revolution by 1795 was at a low ebb.

But men too experienced hardship. Young men were asked to die for the Revolution and more than a million did so, a sacrifice not demanded of women. The disintegration of the family economy in the depressed economic conditions of the second half of the nineties

affected men as well. Some were perhaps more politically compromised than their wives and had had experience in *sociétés populaires* and local politics but that
did not necessarily reconcile them to the hardship and
dislocation of dearth and economic disorder. Those who
had invested hope in the Revolution might attribute
the discomfort to betrayal by the politicians above them
or the people below, but the apathy, hostility, and *esprit
de contrariété* complained about by officialdom during
the Directory was as much male as female. Furthermore, as we have insisted, religion was only one of
several types of manifestation of the spirit of opposition. Gangs of deserters roamed the countryside. Re-
fusals to pay taxes were almost general. The rural
economy was in crisis, which only gradually resolved
itself over the next decade when rents fell. The purchasing power of the rural sector could sustain no industrial revival. In this kind of climate, the failure of
promises and the emptiness of the politicians' rhetoric
were only too apparent. Discontent and defiance of the
Revolution were far from being gender specific.

So why blame religion and elect women as the reason
for the failure of the rational Revolution? First, we must
recognize that republicans could not blame the failure
of the Revolution on the republican record. It was an
uncomfortable fact that republicanism in power had
not worked. A scapegoat had thence to be found if
political credibility was to be maintained. In the political conditions of the nineteenth century the plausibility
and desirability of republicanism were seen to be most
conspicuously challenged by the church. Demolished
during the dechristianizing period of the Revolution,
the reconstruction of this institution seen as so threat-
ening to the existence of republicanism had to be ex-

plained. Napoleon, in the republican view, did not arrive at the Concordat by himself. It was a political necessity forced upon him by counter-revolution. Brooding upon current problems and reading their origins backwards to the Revolution, the republicans in the nineteenth century elected their current enemy, clericalism, as the main reason for their demise in 1795–9 and women as the agents. Present foes became past ones. Women and clerics together incarnated irrationality. The frightening alliance in this view destroyed what we might call first-wave republicanism.

This interpretation was a singularly convenient one. The blame for the collapse of republicanism was shifted away from the politicians and the collapse of the economy in the context of war and dearth. It made possible the contention that irrationality and ignorance undermined reason and science. It appealed to latent misogyny suggesting that an inversion of the natural order in the home was at the root of the problem. It allowed republicans to appropriate to themselves the role of moral crusaders whose earthly Utopia was prematurely terminated.

It is perhaps ironic that both republicanism and Catholicism behind the façade of their polemic stood for the same things. Both wanted moral order, paternal authority, and wifely obedience, responsibility for sexual conduct, and the shunning of excess. However, both constituted a belief system and what severed them was that the deities to whom they proclaimed allegiance were different. Catholicism looked to the supernatural and to an ultramontane influence: republicanism vaunted reason and allegiance to the state, the pursuit of truth through science. Two creeds were then juxtaposed; two deities, God and the state, polarized. Re-

publicans and clericals were engaged in a bitter power
struggle and the temporary loser attributed defeat to
the nurturing of irrationality in home and school. Hence
women's religiosity served as a catch-all for the reasons
for the failure of republicanism to maintain control
when temporarily vested with power in 1793. Michelet
even attributed the failure to pay taxes to bedroom
subversion and hence sought to make women responsible for the economic failures of the Revolution.

The notion of women as the supporters of clericalism
gained in intensity over the nineteenth century and was
further nourished by many other factors. Predominant
amongst these was the failure of republicanism to establish a sound popular base, a fact amply demonstrated in 1848. Clerical power was assumed to be in
the ascendant and nourishing this belief was the burgeoning of religious orders and congregations which
occurred largely after the Napoleonic Concordat of 1801
but which effectively owed its mainspring to actual
decisions made by the government during the Directorial period. The decision to return to *bienfaisance individuelle*, to provide charity, to maintain the hospitals
without effective state monetary support, and to pro-
claim the need for home relief agencies created a space.
To fill it was needed a personnel dedicated to fundraising who would work for relatively little and who
could enter without flinching the hovels of the poor.
Revolutionary rhetoric had not succeeded in providing
willing women – the only people capable in the conditions of the day of assuming such work. Trying not
to see what was happening, and in any case under-
informed at the local level of what was actually going
on, the Directory in fact colluded in the unofficial re-
grouping of the female congregations.[8]

However, it was not possible to function on the shreds of what remained of the congregations which had been starved of recruitment for almost a decade. The sisters who regrouped needed to expand their numbers if they were to make Catholic philanthropy effective, and assertive new orders were needed to take up a heavy burden. We must appreciate the intensity of the spirit of mission which characterized many women of diverse social origins if we are to understand how social Catholicism was reconstructed in the first half of the nineteenth century. This process of reconstruction began in *nonante cinq* when the prison doors opened and the relics of orders and congregations who had refused to take the oath joined the ones who had kept their head down and survived and together they seized the opportunity for a new beginning.

Prison had wearied and undermined some and had taken a death toll. For others the revolutionary experience had been tantamount to a revival of the Christianity of the catacombs. 'Robespierre a peuplé le ciel avec des saints,' wrote Marie Madeleine Postel, who was to found a new order after the Concordat dedicated to the education of young girls.[9] She and others identified persecution as an opportunity sent from heaven to test the faithful and reaffirm their commitment. Those congregations like the Sisters of Saint Joseph du Puy who had a highly flexible structure and who were firmly integrated with the local populace or those like the *béates* simply resumed their role in the villages and found re-formation relatively easy. The Sisters of Saint Joseph, almost immediately the prison doors were open, began to petition the department for the restitution of what they termed personal property and the property of the poor. They claimed as personal property the houses that some of them had brought into the order as dower. The *béates* had never functioned on a monetary basis but looked to the parish or hamlet which housed them for support in kind – fuel and lentils for the soup pot. This was a service which could be reassumed with the goodwill of the community.

Extraordinary experiences which were the result of revolutionary dislocation prompted a number of women to form incipient new congregations which later received formal recognition. Anne Marie Rivier was one such woman. At Thueyts in the Vivarais, from 1795, she replaced the curé for purposes such as baptism, ran a school and catechized the young, and formed a group of young women who did the same kind of work in neighbouring parishes.[10] A decade later, her congregation was formally recognized. The Directory, in proclaiming freedom of teaching in the year III, itself made possible such enterprises for former sisters who could emerge and extend their influence through village schools.

The real growth in the women's orders, however, began after the Concordat and more specifically after 1808 when they were reauthorized and indeed encouraged by both the civil and ecclesiastical hierarchies. Under the First Empire 880 new female congregations were founded.[11] Each congregation began from a mother house which was regionally based though many soon spread and extended their influences to England, Ireland, and North America. Several generations of young Catholics in Boston and Toronto, for example, received their education at the hands of the Sisters of Saint Joseph, whose influence in North America was far to transcend their influence in France.

The numerical strength of the new congregations was

such that by the mid-nineteenth century they exceeded in numbers the entire male secular and regular clergy combined.[12]

The foundation of new congregations owed much to individual widows or spinsters who were usually encouraged by a confessor to develop in a particular direction. The powers of initiative and sense of professional fulfilment made available to women who entered the congregations have prompted a new generation of historians to talk about *le féminisme en religion*.[13] Such a feminism was derived from the notion that women could eschew matrimony, separate themselves from conventional life cycle experience, and dedicate themselves to the creation of a better society. The high proportions of spinsters generated in the sluggish demographic environment of nineteenth-century France and by the loss of an entire generation of young men in the First World War ensured the ongoing strength of these enterprises. Often, in the early decades of the nineteenth century, whilst explicitly dedicated to a task in furtherance of God's work, they emphatically pronounced their triumph over the Revolution. For example, the cleric who nurtured the Soeurs du Sacré Coeur at Brouzils (1814) was the Abbé Monnereau whose father had belonged to the armies of Charette, a Vendéen general. The curé of Foyer, confessor to the foundress of the congregation of Sainte Marie de Torfue in the diocese of Angers, helped the congregation establish itself in 'the very fields where he had done battle with the Mayençais troops.' The defeat of the principles of the Revolution could hardly have been more explicit. In prayers for the repose of the souls of the dead regularly chanted in the houses of the re-emergent congregations, a martyrology of priests and confessors was intoned which kept alive clerical suffering during the Revolution.[14]

The new women's orders and the reinvigorated old ones targeted themselves at the resolution of three basic issues: the education of the young and hence the production of the Catholics of the future; the alleviation of the sick and help for the handicapped, and support services to relieve the populace of certain problems. The last could include crèche services for working mothers, the provision of layettes for poor families where the mother guaranteed to breast-feed her baby, and retreats and religious instructions for specific sections of the population. Young servant girls, for example, were frequently singled out as needing a spiritual retreat for a few days per year. For the girls, the experience was of a workbreak with meals and peer group companionship but this experience was placed within a context of confession, discussion, and communal worship. Some orders ran dormitories to protect young immigrant workers in the towns and, most significant, the congregations became, as they had been under the old regime, involved in teaching working skills and running textile workshops. The scale of these enterprises, however, was dramatically extended.

An immense amount of inspiring and valuable work is now being done on the relationships between social Catholicism, socialism, and republicanism which cannot be reviewed here. Republicans and radicals embroiled in struggles with the church saw the strength of the congregations and feared their hold over the population. They readopted enlightenment arguments about the ascendancy achieved over the poor through the distribution of private welfare and gradually sought to construct state alternatives. The most bitter verbal and political battles were fought over education. It was alleged that the church's influence over education produced *deux jeunesses*, the one educated by the church and the other by the state. They assigned women collectively to the church category. They shuddered at what they interpreted as an acculturation process for women which was hostile to the republican tradition and its rational scientific base, a process which included a history of the Revolution as a diabolic republican failure. They opened Catholic history books and found reference to the anarchy that followed the destruction of the old regime and accounts of the martydom of specific faithful and the evil doings and godlessness of certain men. If they ever picked up *vie édifiantes*, lives of saints and martyrs who lived during the Revolution, they would have found the female saint set in a world of evil bureaucrats, and forced to live under the shadow of the guillotine. She holds on to her beliefs. Bad and good appear in the guise of the Revolution, promoted by an impious bourgeoisie of Protestant tendencies, on the one hand, and the good is upheld by a fragile, tenacious Catholic woman on the other. Cultural feminism has rarely had a more assertive formulation because the female, good though physically weak, triumphs and leads the way to a better and more harmonious order.

Both republicans and the Catholic church had a vested interest in interpreting the Revolution to forward their particular ends. Both played with the facts. One would never, for example, appreciate from the Catholic tradition the degree to which the church was brought back by the populace from below;[15] one would never learn from the republican and socialist tradition how disastrous the first experiments in state welfare had proved to be. In the late nineteenth century and the first years of the twentieth when efforts were being made to improve state welfare services, republicans and socialists wrote gloomy histories of the inadequacy of old regime relief and idealized the efforts of the revolutionaries. Catholic historians for their part, dwelt on the failures of the Revolution.[16] In the context of the bitter struggles between the two protagonists, objectivity was little valued.

The persuasion that the church was strengthening its hold and would never, unless drastic action were taken to reformulate the acculturation process of women, cease to pose a threat was one widely held by political radicals but not confirmed by evidence. The registers recording religious observance which formed the basis of the work of a distinguished school of religious sociologists under the leadership of Gabriel le Bras and le Chanoine de Boulard show that by the second half of the nineteenth century, the church had lost control of the minds and practices of more than a significant minority of both men and women. The devotional map of France in the nineteenth century was extremely variegated. There continued to be areas of piety, such as Brittany and Franche Comté, where female observance was the norm for over 60 per cent of the population, but far greater geographical areas where the norm hovered between 20 and 60 per cent and *pays de mission* (areas where only a minority of the population fulfilled their spiritual obligations and in which cities such as Paris and Marseilles and textile areas such as Troyes and the cities of the Nord predominated). Here, less than 20 per cent of women could generally be found who practised regularly, but within these areas there were significant local exceptions, particularly in the Midi. Dramatic contrasts could exist, as they did in Flanders, between the performance of rural women and that of women in textile cities and towns where slippage amongst women was not far behind that of men. Between the extremes of piety and indifference lay areas of seasonal conformity where the majority of the population were baptized, married, and buried within the bosom of mother church and fulfilled their Easter duties, but where weekly attendance at mass was faltering. In pious and impious areas the gap between the performance of men and women was relatively narrow. Even so, in summarizing the record, François Le Brun suggests that we think in terms of three out of every four church goers in this period as being women.[17] We should also think of the church as losing souls (if not necessarily to republicanism). By 1830 it was possible to discern the degree to which the church had not recovered from the Revolution. Only 10 per cent of those in the Parisian Basin and as few as 6 per cent of those in Versailles practised in 1834, 13 per cent at Orleans in 1852. At the same time about 80 per cent of the west was prepared to go to church and fulfil spiritual obligations.

In spite of missions intended to win back souls for the church, a gradual exodus proceeded apace. With the benefit of hindsight we can appreciate that the republicans had only to wait to realize their hopes of a dechristianized society.[18] They could not, however, feel confident that victory was imminent. Nor was the fear of the triumph of clericalism through women to remain confined to the republicans. In the last two decades of the nineteenth century as French political life became increasingly complex and socialism and feminism became more effective forces, it is striking that both socialist and feminists viewed a woman question with circumspection. For socialism a separate woman question was a detraction from the class struggle of all workers. After early attempts to organize women's labour, activists began to interpret a separate agenda for better wages for women as a marginal issue. Yet there is strong evidence to suggest that women responded enthusiastically to early socialist politicizing and that in the textile cities they not only supported their men but began to form groups demanding fuller political participation. Many were deterred by the male leadership's view that without 'rational' male leadership women's activity could only be erratic and uncontrolled and must be made subservient to male worker activity or channelized into movements for school meals.[19] However, the left, when considering the failure of socialism to penetrate rural France, also found it convenient to blame a home environment where women dominated and were docile to the demands of the church, blatantly overlooking gaps in their own agenda to attract women or their summary treatment of them. Furthermore, in the 1890s when the socialists achieved their own small group in the Chamber and Jean Jaurès became spokesman for the moderate socialists, the socialists progressively asserted themselves, not the republicans, to be the true spiritual legatees of the French Revolution. In this process of appropriation, they became both progressively anticlerical and antifeminist. Significantly, they produced an important and ongoing historiographical tradition of the Revolution which perpetuated the image of woman as religious fanatic and enemy of rational change. Mathiez was perhaps the last truly explicit exponent of this tradition.[20] In short, republicans and socialists here found common ground.

Perhaps even more striking, however, is that much nineteenth- and early twentieth-century French feminism was also shaped by the beliefs either that women were the victims of irrationality and hence if given the suffrage would elect a right-wing clerical assembly or that political power per se was not critical to women if their special roles as women, particularly the role of mother, were appropriately valorized and guaranteed by proper protective legislation. In part, this attitude existed because an important strand in French feminism originated in the republican tradition which was so fixed in its antipathy to clericalism and in part because it imbibed Rousseauist views of the natural differences between the sexes and the special familial role of women.[21] The ideal of Sophie remained untarnished.

A new generation of historians are now concerned to explain why more women continued to valorize religious practice longer than did their menfolk and have, amongst other considerations, urged us to think of the church as employer, as dispenser of welfare, as well as regulator of the rituals governing family life and provider of social outlets for women which they could not find elsewhere.[22] They point out that women were far from docile to the teachings of the church – as the remorseless downward movement of the French birthrate throughout the nineteenth century demonstrates. Above all, they remind us that an absolute commitment to *le dimorphisme sexuel* exceeds the evidence. The trend from 1790 onwards was remorselessly away from the church. In 1796, rural women sought to arrest the process and preserve for themselves and their families what they valorized in religion. Over the next hundred and fifty years they would slip away for reasons which had little to do with the arguments of church and state and much more to do with personal choice. By the time many had made their severance, state services had taken the place of voluntary or church-based philanthropy, alternative forms of sociability existed, and women were able to control their own fertility. When women were given the vote in 1945 in the expectation that this would buttress right-wing and clerical influences, the expectation was not fulfilled. Indeed their exodus from the church accelerated in the postwar decades and there is no evidence to suggest that this would not have been the case had they been given the suffrage earlier.

It is difficult to resist the conclusion that gender emerged as a burning issue between church and political radicalism in the nineteenth century because all parties, particularly the republicans, found it convenient to believe that it was one. It allowed the republicans to masquerade as the party of reason and science and to denounce its opponents as irrational and as the creatures of their womenfolk. In support of the contention, it was always possible to recall a legend. Of only one thing we can be sure: the most persistent ghost of the French Revolution was not the woman of the revolutionary crowds but the counter-revolutionary woman of 1795–6. A citizen at one remove with her rationality called into doubt, she succeeded in becoming the basis of a troubling legend. Her putative control of the private world of home and family – it was held by men and even women of widely differing persuasions – threatened the full flowering of the rational state, the other Eden.

Once again, hysterical, perverse, irrational, unreliable Eve was constructed to explain why man was kept from earthly paradise.

Notes

PREFACE

1 Amongst them, D. Godineau, *Citoyennes Tricoteuses*; A.
Rosa, *Citoyennes*; A. Soprani, *La Révolution et les femmes*
2 As an example of this type of writing J.B. Landes, *Women
and the Public Sphere in the Age of the French Revolution*
3 J. Michelet, *The Women of the French Revolution* (trans. Philadelphia 1855), 152
4 A. Mathiez, *The French Revolution* (Eng. trans London 1929).
Mathiez's political position was to convert Robespierre into a
socialist and hence he absorbed the antifeminist rhetoric of
late 1793.
5 Mathiez and Aulard probably got most of their vocabulary
for describing women's activities from the *Correspondance
officielle des représentants en mission et le registre du Conseil
exécutif provisoire*, which Aulard edited.
6 In conversation with the author at Grinnell College, Iowa,
September 1989.

CHAPTER 1

1 N.G. Rudé, *The Crowd in the French Revolution*
2 S. Desan, 'Crowds, Community and Ritual in the Work of E.P. Thompson and Nathalie Davis,' in *The New Cultural History*, ed. Lynn Hunt, 47–71, gives a good bibliography.
3 C. Lucas, 'The Crowd and Politics between Ancien Régime and Revolution in France,' *Journal of Modern History* 60/3 (1989), 421–55
4 G. Lefebvre, 'Foules révolutionnaires,' in *Etudes sur la Révolution française* (Paris 1934), 371–92, first gave a specialized definition to the crowd of the *journées* as one which carried the Revolution into a further political phase.
5 R.C. Cobb, *The Police and the People*, and K. Tønnesson, *La Défaite des sans-culottes*
6 J. Flammermont, ed., *La Journée du 14 juillet 1789: Fragment de mémoires inédits de L.G. Pitra* (Paris 1892), 13, 22
7 The best account of the October Days, in spite of its evident antipathy to the women involved, is to be found in the text and even more in the footnotes of Dom Leclerq, *Les Journées d'octobre*, which far exceeds in richness A. Mathiez, 'Etude critique des journées des 5 et 6 octobre 1789' *Revue Historique* lxvii, lxviii, and lxix (1898–9), which forms the basis of Rudé's account in *The Crowd and the French Revolution*. Apart from an uncritical reliance on the *Procédure criminelle instructé au Châtelet de Paris sur la dénonciation des fait arrivés à Versailles dans la journée du 6 octobre 1789* (Paris 1790), a spurious attempt by the Constituent Assembly to reconcile the fury of the king at the treatment of himself and his family on that night, with their own abhorrence of the crowd, on the one hand, with their recognition that much had been achieved to their advantage, on the other, Leclerq's study leaves no attempt to uncover evidence unexamined and in spite of his detestation of the women involved, he does not distort the facts. Contemporaries of all political hues, includ-

ing Maillard who led the women, Lafayette, Bailly, the mayor of the commune, deputies such as Mounier and de Ferrieres, the queen's retinue which included Madame de Campan and courtiers like Madame de la Tour du Pin, and observers like the bookseller Hardy and the writer Sébastien Mercier, are but a few of those who observed at first hand some part of the events. No one, however, witnessed the entire proceedings and some applied in retrospect a gloss to their accounts in order to justify their respective roles. The author intends to make a collection of the accounts as the event still demands the approach of the detective. Of the recent general histories of women in the revolution, Anne Soprani's *La Révolution et les femmes*, 27–40, examines in particular the role of Reine Audu and whether or not Théroigne de Mericourt was present and uses, amongst others, the descriptions of Madame de Stael, anxious over the life of her father, Necker.

8 *Mémoires de Bailly* (Paris 1822), tome iii, p 406: 'Déposition de Maillard sur les évènements du 5 et du 6 octobre'

9 According to Rivarol, *Mémoires* (Paris 1962), Reine Audu alone brought along eight hundred women who joined the main force at Sèvres.

10 Le Baron Marc de Villiers, *Reine Audu*, 22–7

11 It would seem that a delegation of half that size was in fact sanctioned.

12 Michelet is committed to accentuating the non-violence of women's participation but at the level of fact – rather than interpretation – he is almost invariably reliable.

13 A. Mathiez, *Etude critique des journées* ..., gives the most systematic coverage of reaction to this issue. For Madame de Tourzel, the events of this evening were totally distorted by 'factious spirits' who 'feigned the greatest anxiety in regard to the results of a banquet which, so they said, was only the prelude to a counter-revolution. They then succeeded in organizing a movement sufficiently violent to compel the king to go to Paris and consummate more easily the execution of

their designs ...' (*Memoires of the Duchess de Tourzel* [London 1886], 26).

14 On the timing of marketing grain, O. Hufton, 'Social Conflict and the Grain Supply in Eighteenth-Century France,' in R. Rotberg and T.K. Rabb, eds, *Hunger and History* (Cambridge 1985), 105–35.

15 'The men are hanging back ...; the men are cowards ...; tomorrow things will go better; we shall lead.' Such expressions recur as a prelude to all the women's journées. A. Lasserre, *Participation collective des femmes à la Révolution française*, summarizes this activity by the statement 'les hommes suivirent l'impulsion des femmes.' Villers, 10–11, gives further examples of the 'warm-up' to these *journées*.

16 These and less favourable titles appear in the *Procédure criminelle* ...; the recent attention given the impending bankruptcy on the part of the government and the debate on the constitution in which the extent of the king's power was in question which was to continue into the next year as a burning issue explain the mode of reference. The queen is made responsible for financial disaster and the political powers of her husband are seen as exercised by her. She is capable of subversion in the home of Versailles.

17 These mysterious women appear only in royalist accounts intent on demonstrating that ignorant women were duped by women not of their class who were probably in adulterous intrigues with specified factions. They appear in Leclerq's narrative.

18 S. Hardy, *Mes loisirs*

19 As a schoolchild in the 1950s this was the rendering of the October Days that came my way.

20 A passive citizen was one who, under the constitution which was debated, was not allowed the suffrage because he paid under three days' labour in taxes. Historians have dedicated a great deal of effort to demonstrating that the evolving popular militant of the sections of Paris, the *sans-culotte*, was in fact not usually a passive citizen. However, such studies

tend to focus on the leadership and we have no evidence that it was the evolving *sans-culotte* leadership involved in these *journées*. The men and women were drawn from those *quartiers* like the faubourg Saint Antoine where the number of passive citizens was high. Clearly the National Guard does not fit into this category.

21 R.C. Cobb, 'The Revolutionary Mentality in France,' *History* 146 (1957), 3–46. I wrote my first piece on women in the Revolution in 1968 by trying to give the man he describes in this piece a wife.

22 The phrase *les bienfaits de la Révolution* appears constantly in the discourse generated in 1789. The benefits accruing from the Revolution were usually defined as spiritual rather than crassly material.

23 Although their arguments were couched in generic terms, it is clear from the actions of these groups, and their alliance with the Girondins who were elected according to a property qualification, that they did not envisage the rights of full citizenship for the women of the masses. No one was more afraid of the women of the revolutionary crowd than Mary Wollstonecraft who was at this time writing *The Vindication of the Rights of Women* in virtual isolation in Paris. There is no evidence to show that she ever met Olympe de Gouges or the other club leaders.

24 This story is well told in Elizabeth Roudinesco's remarkable biography of Théroigne de Méricourt, *Une femme mélancolique sous la Révolution*.

25 Bibliothèque Nationale, Mss. N.A. 2660

26 D. Godineau, *Citoyennes Tricoteuses*, provides a remarkable, passionate, and learned study of the relationship between the organized club and the militant women of the crowds. She is rightly insistent that the club should not be seen as *un sous produit enragé*. Whilst acknowledging this, we have to be aware that the perception of the politicians was of a linkage between the women and the *enragés*.

27 From February 1793, the price of bread was fixed at three

sous the pound, subsidized by the state. See the works of Susan Petersen, 'Les Femmes dans les files d'attente,' in *Les Femmes et la Révolution française*, ed. M.F. Brive, 86–94, and *Marktweiber und Amazonen: Frauen in der französischen Revolution* (Köln 1987), 121–50.

28 *Moniteur*, 26 February 1793

29 Voyer d'Argenson, *Journal* (Paris 1891) vii p. 425

30 For de Méricourt the event is held to have precipitated bouts of melancholia and the onset of dementia. Simon Schama uses her subsequent drawn-out incarceration in mental hospitals until her death in 1817 as symbol and metaphor for the compulsions of revolutionary idealism: *Citizens: A Chronicle of the French Revolution* (New York 1989), 874–5.

31 Isnard, *Journal des Amis* no. 16, 25 May 1793

32 *Journal de la Convention* no 58, 25 May 1793

33 Tuetey, *Réportoire* ..., ix no 606

34 'A group of women styling themselves revolutionaries, a troop of savages, thirsting for blood.'

35 Godineau, *Citoyennes Tricoteuses*, 150–1, and J. Guilhaumou, 'Description d'un évènement discursif: la mort de Marat à Paris,' in *La mort de Marat*, ed. J.C. Bonnet (Paris 1986). Here the entire relationship of blood and symbolism of fecundity is abundantly discussed.

36 *Moniteur*, 28 August 1793; the address was also published as a pamphlet on 12 September.

37 Note again the use of the verb *traîner* in the sense of to malinger. M. Cerati, *Le Club des Citoyennes Républicaines Révolutionnaires* (Paris 1966), 86.

38 Even in the spring of 1793, *enragé* rhetoric had included allusions to the strength of female protest movements; for example, Varlet (16 March) in the Convention openly wished 'que l'apathie des Jacobins soit remplacée par l'énergie des femmes des 5 et 6 octobre' (Arch. Nat., AF iv 1470).

39 M. Dommanget, *Jacques Roux et le Manifeste des Enragés* (Paris 1948), 55

40 This philosophy had informed the piecemeal market inci-

dents of February 1793 and may explain the hostility of market women to the *enragés*. These women had previously, as on October 5 and 6, been part of the traditional pattern of protest. Hence the old tradition was severed from new developments.

41 This institution, studied by R.C. Cobb, *Les Armées Révolutionnaires* (trans. M. Elliot, *The People's Armies* [London 1989]), was intended to force subsistences out of and patriotism upon the provinces and was formed of local patriots designated by the *sociétés populaires*. It became the most hated of all the institutions imposed upon rural France by Paris.

42 W. Markov, ed., *Roux: Acta et Scripts ...*, 126

43 Tuetey, *Répertoire ...*, ix 1337

44 *Moniteur*, 21 September 1793

45 R.B. Rose, *The Enragés: Socialists of the French Revolution?* A review of this work by R.C. Cobb in *A Second Identity* (Oxford 1969), 168–76, denies that they can be distinguished from the *sans-culottes* militants or the *hébertistes* by drawing lines of ideological demarcation. He defines his followers in purely socio-economic terms: 'Auvergnat water carriers, Savoyard chimney sweeps, market porters, builders' apprentices ... journeymen carpenters, coal heavers, river workers, categories that had no stake in the Revolution and that hardly impinged on the so called "popular movement" that of the *sans-culottes militants*. They were not householders: they remained, even in 1793–4, as sub-citizens with military service as their only "right" and with no one other than Roux to speak up for them' (Cobb, *Second Identity ...*, 170). If the women they organized to take part in the grocery riots were drawn from the same socio-economic grouping, we would not expect to find them in the Club des citoyennes républicaines révolutionnaire. Furthermore, the hostility of a part of the leadership to association with the *enragés* might be attributable to a desire to distance themselves from what they discerned as an undesirable gang of thugs and riff-raff.

Robespierre's smear campaign against Roux consisted of stressing the hostility between him and Marat, who, as we have seen, had enjoyed mystical pre-eminence in the club's esteem.

46 Chabot, *Journal historique et politique*, no 69, 18 September 1793

47 B. Rose, *The Enragés*, 63, and, A. Soboul, 'Une épisode des luttes populaires en septembre 1793: la guerre des cocardes,' *Annales Historiques de la Révolution Française* (1961), 52–5

48 J.P. Amar, *à la Convention, séance du 9 brumaire an II*, Le Moniteur Universel, xviii, 1 November 1793

49 Susan Peterson, 'Les Femmes dans les files d'attente ...,' 194

50 *The armées révolutionnaires* were suppressed on 7 germinal an II (27 March 1794). In the six months of their existence, they had succeeded in alienating much of provincial France from the policies of the central government.

51 O. Hufton, *Bayeux in the Late Eighteenth Century*, 224–5, recounts the experience of one small town.

52 Archives Nationales F7 4766d Marguerite Laroche: 'The time will come when the deputies will be branded on the forehead with hot irons (the mark of a criminal under the old regime) ..., we will go to the Convention and disband them at gunpoint.'

53 Archives Nationales F7 2499. The verb *traîner* (to lag or drag one's feet) is particularly common as is the implication of male cowardice.

54 Archives Nationales F7 4582. Déclaration de Canton. The use of the word *couillon* (cuckold) to pour aspersions on a feeble man attempting to assert his manliness is absolutely classic in the vocabulary of insults.

55 Godineau, *Citoyennes Tricoteuses ...*, 319–42, in the most moving section of the book, gives the best anatomy of prairial which she sees as the apogee of women's political action in the context of the Revolution.

56 Neither Godineau nor Tønnesson deals in numbers.

57 S. Delacroix, *La Réorganisation de l'Eglise de France après la Révolution*. This religious revival was relatively short-lived. Within twelve months only women and the old presented themselves regularly for confession.

58 On this issue, R.C. Cobb, *Death in Paris, 1795–1801*. There do not appear to have been more female suicides than male.

59 Godineau, *Citoyennes Tricoteuses* ..., 337

60 Godineau, *Citoyennes Tricoteuses* ..., 339–40, gives other examples of how defences for women were often based on charges that they had been exposed to propaganda and because they were frail and ignorant had ceded to the persuasion. This was a traditional ploy to escape punishment but it also accorded with the image that the authorities wished to promote of an irrational woman who was a troublemaker because she could not distinguish truth from imposture.

61 'I could not preserve myself from the ascendancy that apparently patriotic imposters gained over me. I believed that in ceding to their lies and insinuations I was serving my country as my husband and sons served it in the army.' This defence embodied allusions to the credulous and gullible woman who was basically well intentioned stripped of the support of male figures who were absent on the business of the state.

62 The terms of this decree are themselves revelatory: 'Des femmes ou égarées ou suscitées par les ennemis de la liberté abusent des égards qu'on a pour la faiblesse de leur sexe, courent les rues, s'attroupent, se mettent dans les rangs et jettent le désordre dans toutes les opérations des police et militaires, décrète que toutes les femmes se retireront, jusqu'autrement soit ordonné, dans leurs domiciles respectifs; celles qui, une heure après l'affiche du présent decret, seront trouvées dans les rues, attroupées au dessus de cinq, seront dispersées par la force armée et successivement mises en arrestation.'

63 Archives Nationales F11 1183. This pronouncement was next extended to 'femmes militaires invalides leur domicile

de droit est toujours le domicile de leurs maris; ainsi a quelq'époque qu'elles sont venues à Paris, elles suivent la condition de leur époux et n'ont point d'autre domicile que leurs époux.' If abandoned or divorced, they had to leave the capital.

CHAPTER 2

1 Very few, clerical marriages (in fact the available evidence suggests that no more than 4.5 per cent of them) were to ex-nuns; C. Langlois and J.T.A. Le Goff, 'Pour une sociologie des prêtres mariés,' *Voies nouvelles pour l'histoire de la Révolution française*, colloque Albert Mathiez–Georges Lefebvre (Paris 1978), 302.

2 O. Hufton and F. Tallett, 'Communities of Women, the Religious Life and Public Service in 18th Century France,' in M. Boxer and J. Quaertert, eds., *Connecting Spheres* (Oxford 1987), 74–85

3 On poverty and its relief during the Revolution the point of departure must be C. Bloch, *Procès Verbaux et Rapports du Comité de Mendicité de la Constituante, 1790–1791,* and A. Tuetey, *L'Assistance publique à Paris pendant la Révolution;* M. Bouchet, *L'Assistance publique en France pendant la Révolution;* L. Lallemand, *La Révolution et les pauvres* and *Histoire des enfants abandonnés et délaissés;* L. Parturier, *L'Assistance publique à Paris sous l'ancien régime et pendant la Révolution.* Although these are old and partisan studies and their date of publication should be noted since they occur in the midst of the debates on public welfare and the church in the anticlerical atmosphere which led up to the separation of church and state in 1905, they still have much to offer. More recent studies which include the experience of the poor are: O. Hufton, *Bayeux in the Late Eighteenth Century;* C. Jones, *Charity and 'Bienfaisance';* A. Forrest, *The French Revolution and the Poor.*

4 Archives Nationales M672 and O. Hufton, *The Poor of Eighteenth Century France,* 159

5 C. Bloch, *Procès verbaux* ..., 346; see also Hufton, *The Poor of Eighteenth Century France*, 332.

6 L. Lallemand, *Les Enfants abandonnés et délaissés*, passim, is particularly eloquent, in light of the subsequent record, of the irony of this nomenclature.

7 There is something of an irony in the situation. The state became, as it were, the father of every abandoned illegitimate child but was to prove a very inadequate one. The change resulted from a 'rational' appraisal during the Revolution of an ancien régime irrationality and barbarity. The feminists who attacked the change a hundred years later wanted more state intrusion on behalf of mothers even if history had taught them that the rational state was unlikely to deliver the funds. Emanating from the Republican tradition which idealized the Revolution, the reforming women notwithstanding identified this piece of legislation as deleterious to the family.

8 Lallemand, *Les Enfants abandonnés* ..., particularly chapter 11

9 O. Hufton, *The Poor* ..., 342

10 C. Bloch and A. Tuetey, *Procès verbaux et rapports du Comité de Mendicité de la Constituante, 1790–91*. The questionnaire and the limited responses appear on pages 568–71.

11 C. Bloch, *L'Assistance et l'Etat en France à la veille de la Révolution*, 4–5. Whilst gathering together the procès verbaux, Bloch found scraps of paper with sums on them to try to make realistic estimates but since none of the conclusions appeared in the remaining work of the comité, he assumed that the members despaired. Another interpretation might be that they became alarmed at the direction in which such calculations were leading.

12 O. Hufton, 'Women wihout Men: Widows and Spinsters in Britain and France in the 18th Century,' *Journal of Family History*, Winter 1984: 351–2.

13 M. Bouloiseau, 'Aspects sociaux de la crise cotonnière dans les campagnes rouennaises en 1778–9 ,' *Actes du 82e Congrès des Sociétés Savantes*, 414; P. Deyon, 'Le Mouve-

ment de la production textile à Amiens,' *Revue du Nord*, xliv (1962), 201–11; G. Gulickson, *Spinners and Weavers of Auffray*, 87–91

14 Many socio-economic historians have regarded the estimates made by the Comité de Mendicité as a chronic underestimate of the real situation. For example, G. Lefebvre, *Etudes Orléanaises* (Paris 1962), vol 1, 218–19 and *Les Paysans du Nord*, 308–9; for a comparative bibliography, Hufton, *The Poor* ..., 24 n. 1.

15 For example, A. Cobban, *A History of Modern France* (London 1957), 176, and N. Hampson, *The First European Revolution, 1776–1815* (London 1969), 90–1.

16 This statement is not to make a plea for the adequacy of the hotchpotch of agencies according relief under the old regime but to promote the realization that what was proposed here was no better and potentially worse.

17 I first used this phrase in my work *The Poor* ..., 69–107.

18 One response to this problem is outlined in Hufton, *Bayeux* ..., 97. The opposition of the sisters in this respect, unfortunately in this town, secured them the personal antipathy of the surgeon who was to be the town's mayor during the Revolution. At least, however, he had a respect for human life and his revenge was limited.

19 Archives Nationales s6174

20 The case involving the sister of Saint Joseph du Puy at Chaise Dieu (cited above) may in fact have related to a former sister of the congregation who in death was reclaimed by the congregation.

21 Hufton, *Bayeux* ..., 181

22 Some of the incidents and extracts describing them in the gutter press are found in a curious work written under the pseudonym of Jean de Villiot entitled *La Flagellation amoureuse dans la littérature; suivie de la flagellation des femmes en France sous la Révolution et la terreur blanche* (Paris 1904), 204. The work has a voyeur quality but the evidence used is accurate for the Revolution and the work – without ex-

pressly making the point – does show how women could be used or take it upon themselves to bring women to account. They are the first judge of their sex. This perhaps makes explicable the flagellation of Théroigne de Méricourt.

23 Michelet, *The Women of the French Revolution* ..., 165

24 The history of the *congrégations* during the Revolution remains to be written. The task will not be easy because they were operating on the other side of the law. Interest in the *congrégations* and their subversive nature was acknowledged at the beginning of this century when the struggle between church and state was at its height: e.g. A. Aulard, *La Révolution française et les congrégations*. Some of the orders and congregations have individual if not often amateur histories: e.g., A. Bois, *Les Soeurs de Saint Joseph,* and F. Groult, *Une Congrégation Salésienne.*

25 C. Jones, 'The Politics and Personnel of Social Welfare,' *Beyond the Terror* ..., 86, and Hufton, *Bayeux* ..., 245

26 Many instances are given in L. Lallemand, *La Révolution et les Pauvres*, 121–53.

27 Hufton, *Bayeux* ..., 247; R.C. Cobb, 'Disette et mortalité à Rouen,' *Terreur et subsistances*, 329

28 Archives Nationales F15 274 *Administrateurs et l'hospice de l'humanité au Ministre*

29 Archives Nationales F15 283 *La Commission administrative*

30 Archives Nationales F15 292 *Le Bureau des hospices*

31 Archives Nationales F15 351 *Hospices*

32 Louis Parturier, *L'Assistance à Paris sous l'ancien régime et pendant la Révolution.* Some of the new institutions like the comités de bienfaisance survived until well into the nineteenth century.

33 Bibliothèque Nationale Lb40 1772 (microfiche) Section Champs Elysées 21 Septembre 1793

34 Archives Nationales F15 2871, *Commission Centrale de Bienfaisance thermidor an* II

35 I was struck when examining the municipal registers of the period of the terror at le Puy en Velay, for example, how

Solon Reynaud, whose terrorist activities will be presently discussed, did not seem to have much difficulty in raising loans.

36 R.C. Cobb, *Reactions to the French Revolution*, 143

CHAPTER 3

1 The most recent essay in this direction, F. Aftalion, *The French Revolution: An Economic Interpretation* (Cambridge 1990), is a study of policy rather than an in-depth study of the economic consequences of the Revolution.

2 M. Bouloiseau, 'Aspects de la crise contonnière dans les campagnes rouennaises en 1789–1790,' *Actes du 82e congrès des sociétés savantes*, 414; M. Garden, *Lyon et les Lyonnais au XVIIIe siècle*, 302; P. Wolff, ed., *Histoire de Languedoc* (Toulouse 1967), 404–6; P. Deyon, 'Le Mouvement de la production textile à Amiens,' *Revenue du Nord*, xliv (1962), 201–11; J. Kaplow, *Elbeuf during the Revolutionary Period* (Baltimore 1964), 39–51; G. Gulickson, *Spinners and Weavers of Auffray*, 69; O. Hufton, *The Poor of Eighteenth-Century France*, 17–38

3 R. Beaudun, 'Le Mouvement de prix, des salaires et les révoltes populaires à Lyon de 1760 à 1790' (Diplôme d'Etudes Supérieures, Lyon 1962)

4 Archives Municipales Bayeux, *Registre des Délibérations 2–3 floréal an* III 'When God was there we had bread.'

5 The saying 'Men make laws, women customs' was often evoked in the nineteenth century and interpreted as a reason for clerical influence. The clergy themselves had recourse to the saying as a means of urging upon the female laity the extent of their influence: e.g., Donnet, archbishop of Bordeaux, in his *Instruction pastorale sur l'éducation de famille* (1845), J.P. Migne, *Collection intégrale et universelle des orateurs sacrés*, 99 vols, vol 81, 69.

6 R.C. Cobb, *The Police and the People*, 50–2. This entire section of Cobb's work should be obligatory reading for anyone who wants to comment seriously on the meaning of dis-

course. The official makes even porters and fishwives declaim in the language of *la rhétorique*. The simple phrase 'merde à la Convention' can thus be stretched to a twelveline paragraph. The more words one used and the more paper covered, the more assiduous the official appeared. Since officials acted as the filters of popular discourse, we cannot ever be sure exactly what the people were saying.

7 Examples taken from the Archives Départementales de la Haute Loire L430, 371, 1206

8 'Females, little women, bigots, animals, woolly beasts, sheep, lentils, vegetables, fanatics.' The use of the term *lentilles* was obviously specific to an area like the Haute Loire where there were a staple. Certainly women, in this discourse, were what they ate.

9 This was the official phrase for dechristianization.

10 An example of this questionnaire is found in J. Hardman, *French Revolution Documents* (Oxford 1973), 173.

11 If such a notion could be proved, it would lend a particular twist to the legend of the priest supported by women which developed in the nineteenth century. However, the record of women as supporters of the priest during the years 1789–93 probably constitutes the decisive evidence which serves to undermine the idea.

12 M. Vovelle, *La Révolution contre l'Eglise*, 221–6

13 'These buildings will only contain the voices of republicans instructing their brothers and manly accents of patriotism honouring reason.' Section de Gravilliers; cited in Hardman, *Documents*, 369–70. There seems to be little space here for sisters' or women's voices.

14 On the bewildering religious commitment of the *sans-culotte*'s wife, F. Le Brun, ed., *Histoire des Catholiques en France du XVe siècle jusqu'à nos jours*.

15 In the early winter of 1794, a so-called *sans-culottes* paternoster circulated which suggests that women were not the only ones to maintain some allegiance to a deity if not to its priesthood. 'Our Father who art in heaven whence you pro-

tect the French Republic and the *sans-culottes*, its most ardent defenders, let your name be hallowed amongst us as it has always been. May thy will to let man live free, equal and happy be done on earth as it is in heaven. Preserve our supply of daily bread threatened by the efforts of Pitt Cobourg and the coalition of tyrants. Forgive us the errors committed by tolerating for so long the tyrants now purged from France. As we forgive the enslaved nations when they intimidate us. Let them not delay too long in casting off their shackles ... May they be delivered like us from nobles, priests and kings. Amen.' Cited by Hardman, *Documents*, 367.

16 On these differences before the Revolution, O. Hufton, 'The French Church,' 13–33.

17 The oath of allegiance was not initially envisaged when the first legislation on the civil constitution of clergy which converted the priesthood into salaried officials of the state, reduced the number of bishops, abolished many cathedral canonries, and made all appointments subject to lay election was enacted. It was only perceived as necessary when it became clear that many clerics – at first about half and subsequently more – were fundamentally opposed to the principles it embodied. Perhaps the most alienating aspect was that of lay election which represented a total breach of the autonomy of the church. In diocesan centres where seminaries existed, the theological implications of the oath were hotly debated and parish priests, who may well have welcomed becoming state salaried employees on a generous stipend, recoiled before the wider implications of state control. They then explained to their flocks the reasons for their rejection of the oath. The clergy hence became the first really explicit oppositional Revolution. T. Tackett, *Religion, Revolution, and Regional Culture in Eighteenth Century France*; the particular opposition of women is outlined on 172–7.

18 Archives Départementales Calvados Lv Liasse de Serments Bayeux. 'Take it or not, it doesn't bother us.'

19 T. Tackett, *Religion, Revolution* ..., 175, and *Priest and Parish in Eighteenth Century France* (Princeton 1977), 192

20 Chanoine Pierre Flament, 'Recherche sur le ministre clandestin dans le département de l'Orne sous la Révolution,' *Bulletin de la Société historique et archéologique de l'Orne* xc (1972), 45–74; E. Gonnet, *Essai sur l'histoire du diocèse du Puy en Velay*, 209; Charles Girault, *Le Clergé Sarthois face au serment constitutionel*, 31–3

21 René and Suzanne Pillorget, 'Les Messes clandestines en France entre 1793 et 1802,' 155–67. This work has a valuable bibliography of local and other published work on this elusive subject.

22 *Actes du Comité de Salut Public*, i p 353, and R. and S. Pillorget, 'Les Messes clandestines en France,' 160

23 *Moniteur*, 19 Messidor an II. I am indebted to Carol Blum for this reference.

24 Cited by M. Vovelle, *La Révolution contre l'Eglise*, 224

25 The White Terror was a terrorist movement which broke out after 1795 in the Midi. It was directed against former partisans of the Terror and hence could be called a counter-Terror. Essentially it was a movement designed to wreak revenge for loss of life or unpopular policies and some aspects of it will presently be discussed. On this theme and for many nuances in this movement: C. Lucas, 'Themes in Southern Violence after 9 Thermidor,' in *Beyond the Terror*, ed G. Lewis and C. Lucas, 152–94. The case from Arles appears in M. Vovelle, *Les Métamorphoses de la fête en Provence*, 251.

26 The designation 'macho' is used deliberately because the rhetoric of officialdom demanded admiration for the rational male who could alone make decisions. The female symbol of Liberty was removed from official correspondence after the end of 1793 and replaced by the symbol of Hercules, manly vigour, because a female symbol suggested weakness. The indelicacy and lack of consideration demonstrated by both local officials and the *armées révolutionnaires* towards niceties

appreciated by women are illustrated in an incident from Saint Germain de Laval in the Maçonnais wherein local Jacobins took a classical nude statue from a local chateau and painted a tricolore on her and stood her in the square having felled a crucifix, proclaiming her the Goddess of Liberty. Days later it began to rain and the paint started to wash off and descended in a purplish red trickle between her legs. The young men, drunken and jesting, proclaimed a miracle of a menstruating goddess. The village women, outraged, seized the statue, carried her several miles to the river, and washed her, purified her, and restored her dignity as a woman. Then they laid her on her side. A day later they broke into a church and reclaimed it for worship. (Archives Départementales Rhône 42 L161; I am grateful to Colin Lucas for this reference.)

27 I have deliberately confined myself to a particular area and drawn analogies in the notes for coherence.

28 Woods and hedges certainly made for better oppositional activity by young men as the history of the Vendée demonstrates. However, during 1796 even the Beauce, which was flat land not far distant from Orléans and even from Paris, was the locus of banditry which the government could not curtail. See R.C. Cobb, *Reactions to the French Revolution*, 180.

29 She has been designated *un ministre laïque* by a historian of the nineteenth century (A. Rives, 'Des ministres laïques' au XIXe siècle).

30 More often this term was reserved for the *béates* (Archives Départementales, Conseil Général Le Puy 10 October 1793).

31 Rapport du 5 prairial an III, Archives Départementales Haute Loire LB14 (ancien cote), cited in part in Gonnet, *Essai sur l'histoire du diocèse du Puy en Velay* 245–7.

32 Archives Départementales Haute Loire L376 ancien côte

33 Archives Départementales Haute Loire L802 ancien côte

34 This area was a frontier between Catholicism and Protestant-

ism and the Revolution was presented as a Protestant promotion.

35 This case may reflect the reclaiming of a former sister in death as referred to above p. 72.

36 A great deal would seem to have depended upon how secure these local authorities felt as well as their personal predictions. The diocesan histories which are being published by Beauchesne make one aware of very differing levels of tolerance and persecution from area to area.

37 Hufton, 'The Reconstruction of a Church, 1796–1801,' 35

38 Abbé E. Sévestre, *Les problèmes religieux de la Révolution et l'Empire en Normandie*, 1070

39 Abbé P.J.B. Delon, *La Révolution en Lozère*, 52. In the riot of 1790 Rose Bros (née Castan) led the attack on the cathedral chapter's grain supply. She led the movement to hire the church 23 ventose an II (13 March 1795), Delon, 740.

40 M. de Roux, *Histoire de la Révolution à Poitiers et dans la Vienne* (Lyons 1952), 251, and G. Lefebvre, *Les Paysans du Nord*, 874

41 G. Cholvy, *History du diocèse de Montpellier*, 186, for example, states that in the Lodevois in May 1795, 'Les cultes sont librement exercés. Le peuple est appelé aux messes et vèpres par le son de la cloche que l'on met en branle, en outre, trois fois par jour ...'; in Lefebvre, *Les Paysans du Nord*, 874, women occupy bell towers.

42 J. Duval Jouve, *Montpellier pendant la Révolution* (Montpellier 1879), 327

43 'Est-on plus altéré qu'autrefois?' ran a leader article in a Grenoble journal for 1810. The need of the church to extricate men from the tavern on a Sunday became a recurrent preoccupation of the clergy after the Concordat. J. Godel, *La Réconstruction concordataire dans le diocèse de Grenoble*, 266–7.

44 On the eve of the Concordat, the mayor of Lain near Auxerre wrote to the prefect: 'tout le monde est catholique ici ... or un bon tiers des habitants ne veulent plus observer le di-

manche. On reste au cabaret; on joue aux cartes pendant les messes et vèpres; on fauche, on charroie ... nos concitoyens ont toujours tenu une conduite tout a fait opposée à tout ce que la loi prescrit. Pendant l'exercise des jours de décadi tout le monde travaillait ce jour là et célébrait religieusement le dimanche. Aujourd'hui que la décadi est supprimée, on ne veut plus reconnaitre le dimanche.' Cited by H. Forestier, 'Le Culte laïcal,' *Annales de Bourgogne*, xxiv (1952), 107

45 D. Woronoff, *La République bourgeoise de Thermidor à Brumaire*, 143–4, gives a short account of Grégoire's efforts and frustrations. Blind masses have recently been interpreted by S. Desan, *Reclaiming the Sacred*, as an attempt by women to create new rituals. I would prefer to see them as the resurrection of old rituals, as perfect in all details as possible except for the presence of a priest and, even here, the lay celebrant did not intrude upon the prerogatives of the real priesthood by giving communion.

46 Cobb cites the case of one such group walking from Sarrelouis to Meulan in *Police and the People*, 95.

47 Archives Nationales F9 316, Desertion, Tarn, Lautrec, 9 brumaire an VII

48 Cobb, *Police and the People*, 104, and A. Forrest, 'Conscription and Crime in Rural France during the Directory and the Consulate,' in *Beyond the Terror*, ed G. Lewis and C. Lucas, 92

49 C. Lucas, 'Themes in Southern Violence after 9 Thermidor,' in *Beyond the Terror*, ed. G. Lewis and C. Lucas, 152–94

CHAPTER 4

1 O. Hufton, *Bayeux in the Late Eighteenth Century*, 260–4, gives one local example of the fatigue and economic anguish facing officialdom.

2 R.C. Cobb, 'Thermidor or the Retreat from Fantasy,' in H. Lloyd Jones, V. Pearl, and B. Worden, eds, *History and Imagination: Essays in Honour of Trevor Roper* (London 1981), 295

3 C. Jones, 'Picking up the Pieces: The Politics and the Personnel of Social Welfare from the Convention to the Consulate,'
in *Beyond the Terror,* ed G. Lewis and C. Lucas, 53

4 The U-turn implicit in the rhetoric is startling: 'Depuis cette
époque (1790) il semble que tous les speculateurs en bienfaisance aient pris la tache de pousser sans mesure vers le
trésor national toutes les classes du peuple. Qu'est-il arrivé
de ce chaos d'idées? Une serie effrayante de dépenses illi-
mités, des lois stériles et impossibles à exécuter' (cited in
Jones, 60).

5 Archives Départementales Haute Loire L371 (ancien côte) 5
ventôse an VI

6 T. Zeldin, 'The Conflict of Moralities, Confession, Sin and
Pleasure in the Nineteenth Century,' outlines how this
theme was developed as well as the debate within the
French church on what exactly should go in the confessional.

7 'general demoralization, contempt for human life fostered by
revolutionary events, intense economic hardship, extreme
poverty, loss of the habits of work, profound divisions in society, and the timidity and ineffectualness of the forces of
repression' (M. Marion, *Le Brigandage pendant la Revolution*
[Paris 1934]; see also R.C. Cobb, *Reactions to the French Revolution*).

8 Jones, 'Picking up the Pieces,' 81. By 1797 their return was
encouraged by the minister of the interior, who turned a
blind eye to the gradualistic reconstitution of national networks of, for example, the Filles de la Charité. This collusion
finds singularly little admission in subsequent republican
historiography of welfare though the acknowledgment that a
Catholic nursing force of women joined by simple vows
could not be dispensed with before a cadre of lay replacements had been formed was made in the late nineteenth
century on the eve of the severance between church and
state. The unwillingness of the state to repeat the experience
of dispensing with trained nursing sisters in religion in this

period is currently being examined by Katrin Schultheiss of Harvard University.

9 Abbé Delamare, *Vie édifiante de la très honorée supérieure Marie Madeleine née Julie Postel* (Coutances 1852), 9, and Chanoine Claude-Josephe Duchastanier cited by M. de Roux, *Histoire religieuse de la Révolution à Poitiers et dans la Vienne,* 307

10 Le Brun (ed), *Histoire des Catholiques en France du XV siècle à nos jours* (Toulouse 1980), 273. Other examples are given. The *béates* were engaged in the same enterprise.

11 C. Langlois, *Le Catholicisme au féminin.*

12 C. Langlois, 'Les Effectifs des congrégations féminines au XIXe siècle: De l'enquête statistique à l'histoire quantitative,' 54–5. By 1861 women comprised 54 per cent of the personnel of the Catholic church; by 1878, 58 per cent.

13 Y. Turin, *Femmes et religieuses au XIXe siècle*

14 I am indebted to Professor Patricia Byrne, currently engaged in a team project to write the history of the Sisters of Saint Joseph, for calling my attention to this. She pointed out that the Sisters themselves produced martyrs but that their suffering was not commemorated in the litanies which hallowed the memory of the priests. This is perhaps an excellent example of the degree to which the male hierarchy of the Catholic church sought to monopolize the claim to revolutionary martyrdom.

15 The appropriation of the credit for the work of restoration is apparent in many of the diocesan histories produced in the nineteenth century. Generally speaking, the clergy would seem to have controlled the restoration most effectively in the eastern provinces contiguous to Switzerland where they remained in closer contact with their parishes. Hufton, 'The Reconstruction of a Church ...,' 45 and Le Brun, ed., *Histoire des Catholiques en France,* 271.

16 Even Camile Bloch, author of *L'Assistance et l'Etat en France à la veille de la Révolution* and the careful compiler of the documents generated by the Comité de Mendicité, lost much

of his objectivity when he considered Catholic relief. He never broached the question of whether the eighteenth-century French state did have the resources to subsidize up to 20 per cent of its population. On this theme, O. Hufton, *The Poor of Eighteenth Century France, 1750–1789*, 24.

17 F. Le Brun, ed, *Histoire des Catholiques en France*, 322–4, summarizes the work of G. Le Bras, *Etudes de sociologie religieuses* (Paris 1955). He elects the years 1830–50 as those in which the greatest contrasts appear.

18 Ibid 322

19 P. Hilden, *Working Women and Socialist Politics in France, 1880–1914* (Oxford 1986), 270–2, is particularly eloquent on how initial fervour among working women was squandered by a male leadership with conventional views on women's place.

20 Many ambiguities are perforce sacrificed in this quick summary. Until the nineties socialists concentrated on the class rather than the religious struggle. Jaurès himself rationalized his political stance by a belief in compromise with the bourgeoisie. Ironically, his own wife wanted their daughter to receive her first communion, an event which sparked off a lively discussion even at the local level about the appropriateness of this step, women prepared to follow the socialist cause thinking that there was nothing wrong in Mademoiselle Jaurès taking this step. I am indebted to Patricia Hilden for informing me about these discussions.

21 Notably Marie Desraimes, editor of *Le Républicain de Seine et Oise* (1881–5) and organizer of anticlerical congresses in 1881 and 1882

22 G. Cholvy and Y.M. Hilaire, *Histoire religieuse de la France contemporaine*, i: 256–7, stress that in the Midi men and women shared a code of honour in which women's activity outside the home was regarded as safest in the hands of the church, which was an effective guardian of chastity. Caroline Ford, 'Religion and the Politics of Cultural Change in Provincial France: The Resistance of 1902 in Lower Brittany,'

Journal of Modern History March 1990, 11–33, and 'Creating the Nation in Provincial France: Religion and Identity in Brittany' (book ms in preparation), emphasizes that in 1902 both men and women defended the religious institutions most strongly in villages where the Filles du Saint Esprit ran crèche and social services which the state did not replicate. Recent work by Colin Heywood, 'The Catholic Church and the Formation of the Industrial Labour Force in Nineteenth Century France: An Interpretative Essay,' *European History Quarterly*, xix (1989), 509–33, shows how the church as employer, particularly of women and children, could exercise a hold which exceeded the purely religious. Work in progress by Hazel Mills of Fitzwilliam College, Cambridge, demonstrates how the church in the first decades of the nineteenth century began and continued to make a conscious appeal to women in the hope of controlling family behaviour.

Select Bibliography

Abensour, Léon *La Femme et le féminisme avant la Révolution française* Paris 1923

Abray, Jane 'Feminism in the French Revolution' *American Historical Review* 80/1 (February 1975) 43–62

Accarias, L. *L'Assistance publique sous la Révolution dans le département du Puy-de-Dôme* Savenay 1933

Adher, J. *Recueil de documents sur l'assistance publique dans le district de Toulouse de 1789 à 1800* Toulouse 1918

Agulhon, Maurice *Marianne into Battle: Republican Imagery and Symbolism in France, 1789–1880* trans. Janet Lloyd. Cambridge 1981

Albistur, M., and D. Armogathe *Histoire du féminisme français du Moyen Age à nos jours* Paris 1978

Alexandre, Charles A. 'Fragments des Mémoires de ...' ed Jacques Godechot *Annales historiques de la Révolution française* 4 (1952) 146–86

Applewhite, Harriet B., and Darlene Gay Levy 'Ceremonial Dimensions of Citizenship: Women and Oathtaking in Revolutionary Paris' in *Proceedings of the Fifth Rudé Seminar in French History* Wellington, New Zealand, 1986

- 'Responses to the Political Activism of the People in Revolutionary Paris, 1789–1793' in *Women and the Structure of Society: Selected Research from the Fifth Berkshire Conference on the History of Women* ed. Barbara J. Harris and JoAnn K. Mcnamara, 215–31. Durham, NC 1984

- 'Women, Democracy and Revolution in Paris, 1789–1794' in *French Women in the Age of Enlightenment* ed I. Spencer. Bloomington 1984

- 'Women and Political Revolution in Paris' in *Becoming Visible* ed R. Bridenthal and C. Koonz, 279–306. Boston 1988

Arasse, D. *La Guillotine et l'imaginaire de la Terreur* Paris 1987

Ariès, P. *L'Enfant et la vie familiale sous l'Ancien Régime* Paris 1960

Audard, E. *Actes des martyrs et des confesseurs de la foi pendant la Revolution* Tours 1916–20

A. Aulard *Le Culte de la Raison et de l'Etre Suprême, 1793–1794: Essai historique* Paris 1892

- 'Le Féminisme pendant la Révolution' *Revue Bleue* 1898, 361–6

- *Papiers de Fournier l'Américain* Paris 1931

- *Paris pendant la réaction thermidorienne et sous le Directoire* 5 vol. Paris 1898–1902

- *Recueil des Actes du Comité de Salut Public avec la correspondence officielle des représantants en mission et le régistre du Conseil exécutif provisoire* 28 vols. Paris 1881–1915

- *La Révolution française et les congrégations* Paris 1903

- *La Société des Jacobins: Recueil des documents pour l'histoire du Club des Jacobins de Paris* 6 vols. Paris 1889–90

Auteville, M. 'Le Divorce pendant la Révolution' *Revue de la Révolution* 183: 206–473

Badinter, E., *Paroles d'hommes* Paris 1989

- *Qu'est-ce qu'une femme?* Paris 1989

Badinter, E., and R. Badinter *Condorcet* Paris 1988

Bardet, Jean-Pierre 'Enfants abandonnées et enfants assistés à Rouen dans le seconde moitié du XVIIIe siècle' in *Sur la popu-*

lation française aux XVIIIe *et* XIX *siècles* 19–47. Paris 1973

Benabou, E.M. *La Prostitution et la police des moeurs au* XVIIe *siècle* Paris 1987

Berenson, E. *Populist Religion and Left Wing Politics in France, 1830–52* Princeton 1983

Bertaud, J.P. *La Vie quotidienne des soldats de la Révolution française* Paris 1983

– *La Vie quotidienne en France au temps de la Révolution (1789–1799)* Paris 1983

Bertrand-Geoffroy, M. 'Le Culte revolutionnaire et l'opposition à la France dans le département des Alpes Maritimes (1793–1800)' *Actes du Congrès National des Sociétés Savantes,* vol i, 199–209. Paris 1976

Bianchi, S. *La Révolution culturelle de l'an* II: *Elites et peuple, 1789–1799* Paris 1982

Biron, M.P. 'La resistance des laïcs à travers les messes clandestines pendant la Révolution française' *Bulletin de la Société française des idées et d'histoire religieuse* i (1984), 13–37

Blanc, O. *Olympe de Gouges* Paris 1981

Bloch, C. *L'Assistance et l'Etat en France à la veille de la Revolution (1764–1790)* Paris 1908

– 'Les Femmes d'Orléans pendant la Révolution' *La Révolution française* XXXLIII (1902), 49–67

– *Recueil des principaux textes législatifs et administratifs concernant l'assistance de 1789 à l'an* VIII Paris 1909

Bloch, C., and A. Tuetey, eds *Procès-verbaux et rapports du Comité de Mendicité de la Constituante 1790–1791* Paris 1911

Bloch, E. *Droit naturel et dignité humaine* Frankfurt 1961

Bloch, Jean 'Women and Reform of the Nation' in *Women and Society in Eighteenth-Century France* ed E. Jacobs, 3–18. London 1979

Bloch, M., and J. Bloch 'Women and the dialectics of Nature in Eighteenth-Century French Thought' in *Nature, Culture and Gender* ed C.P. MacCormack and M. Strathern, 25–41. Cambridge 1980

Blum, Carol *Rousseau and the Republic of Virtue: The Language of Politics in the French Revolution* Ithaca 1986

Bois, A. *Les Soeurs de Saint Joseph: Les Filles du petit dessin, 1648–*

1949 Le Puy 1949

Bouchet, M. *L'Assistance publique en France pendant la Révolution* Paris 1908

Bouloiseau, M. 'Aspects sociaux de la crise cotnonnière dans les campagnes rouennaises en 1788–1789' in *Actes du 81e Congrès National des Sociétés Savantes, Rouen-Caen, 1956*, 403–28. Paris 1956

Bourdin, I. *Les Sociétés populaires à Paris pendant la Révolution de 1789 jusqu'à la chute de la royauté* Paris 1937

Boussolade, J. *L'Eglise de Paris du 9 thermidor au Concordat* Paris 1950

Boutry, P., and M. Cinquin *Deux pélerinages au XIX siècle: Ars et Paray-le-Monial* Paris 1980

Bouvier, J. *Les femmes pendant la Révolution* Paris 1931

Braesch, F. 'Le marriage civil en octobre 1792' *La Révolution Française* LVI (1909), 221–4

Brive, M.F., ed *Les Femmes et la Révolution française* 3 vols. Colloque de Toulouse 1989; Toulouse 1990–1

Bruller, Jacqueline *Charlotte Corday* Paris 1988

Bruhat, Y. *Les Femmes et la Révolution française* Paris 1939

Buchez, P.B., and B.C. Roux, eds *Histoire parlementaire de la Révolution française, ou Journal des Assemblées nationales depuis 1789 jusqu'au 1815* Paris 1834

Bussière, G. *Etudes historiques sur la Révolution en Périgord* Bordeaux 1897

Caron, P. *Paris pendant la Terreur: Rapports des agents secrets du Ministre de l'Intérieur* Paris 1949

Cerati, Marie *Le Club des Citoyennes Républicaines Révolutionnaires* Paris 1966

Charon-Bordas, Jeannine *La Légation en France du Cardinal Caprara, 1801–1801* Répertoire des demandes de réconciliation avec l'Eglise; Paris 1979

Chassin, Charles-Louis *Les Elections et les cahiers de Paris en 1789* Paris 1888

Cholvy, G. *Histoire du diocèse de Montpellier* Paris 1976

Cholvy, G., and Y. Hilaire *Histoire religieuse de la France Contemporaine* Toulouse 1989

Clawson, Mary Ann 'Early Modern Fraternalism and the Patriarchal Family' *Feminist Studies* 6/2 (summer 1980) 368–91

Cobb, R.C. *Les Armées révolutionnaires* Paris 1961–3; trans. M. Elliott *The People's Armies* London 1989

– *Death in Paris* Oxford 1978

– *The Police and the People: French Popular Protest, 1789–1820* Oxford 1970

– *Reactions to the French Revolution* Oxford 1972

– 'The Revolutionary Mentality in France' *History* 146 (1957) 3–46

– *A Sense of Place* London 1975

– *Terreur et subsistances, 1793–1795* Paris 1964

Condorcet, M. 'On the Admission of Women to the Rights of Citizenship' in Condorcet *Selected Writings* ed K.M. Baker, 97–104. Indianapolis 1976

Coste, P. *Les Filles de la Charité: L'Institut de 1617 à 1800* Paris 1933

– *Livre d'or des Filles de la Charité, ou simple aperçu des plus belles notices des soeurs* Paris 1938

– *Une victime de la Révolution: Soeur Marguerite Rutan, Fille de la Charité* Paris and Lille 1908

Dauxois, Jacqueline *Charlotte Corday* Paris 1989

Dawson, P. ed *The French Revolution* Englewood Cliffs, NJ 1967

Delacroix, S. *La Réorganisation de l'Eglise de France après la Révolution* Paris 1965

Delcambre, E. *La Période du Directoire dans le Haute-Loire* Aubenas 1941

Delon, l'Abbé P.J.B. *La Révolution en Lozère* Mende 1922

Delumeau, J. *Histoire du diocèse de Rennes* Paris 1979

Depauw, J. 'Amour illégitimée à Nantes au XVIIIe siècle' *A.E.S.C.* 229 (July–October 1972) 1155–82

Desan, S. *Reclaiming the Sacred: Lay Religion and Popular Politics in Revolutionary France* Ithaca 1991

Dessertine, D. *Divorcer à Lyon sous la Révolution et l'Empire* Lyon 1981

Devance, L. 'Le Féminisme pendant la Révolution française' *Annales historique de droit français et étranger* (1977) 341–76

Diderot, D. 'On Women' (orig. 1772) in *Dialogues* trans Francis Birrel. London 1927

Dinet, D. 'Les Communautés religieuses féminine de Bourgogne et de la Champagne face à la Révolution' in *Practiques religieuses dans l'Europe révolutionnaire (1770–1820)* Actes du Colloque Chantilly 27–29 Nov. 1986. Paris 1988

Dreyfus, F. *L'Assistance sous la Législative et la Convention (1791–1795)* Paris 1907

Dubois, J. *L'Assistance dans le District de Bar pendant la Révolution* Paris 1930

Duhet, P.M., ed *Cahiers de doléances des femmes en 1789 et autres textes* Paris 1981

Dupuy, R. 'Les Femmes et la Contre-Révolution dans l'Ouest' *Bulletin d'histoire économique et sociale de la Révolution française* 1980: 61–70

Duval, L. 'La Messe de Monsieur des Rotours' *Bulletin de la Société historique et archéologique de l'Orne* 28 (1909) 156–204

– *La Réouverture des Eglises en l'an III dans le District de Bellême* Bellême 1907

Duval-Jouve, J. *Montpellier pendant la Révolution* Montpellier 1879

Elshtain, J.B. 'J.J. Rousseau and Patriarchal Ideology: Liberal Individualism and Motherhood' in *The Radical Future of Liberal Feminism* New York 1981

– *Public Man, Private Woman: Women in Social and Political Thought* Princeton 1981

Ernst, O. *Théroigne de Méricourt* Paris 1935

Evrard, F. 'Les Ouvriers de textile dans la région rouennaise (1789–1802)' *Annales historiques de la Révolution française* 9 (1947) 333–52

Farge, A. *Le Miroir des femmes; textes de la Bibliothèque Bleue* Paris 1982

– *La Vie fragile, pouvoirs et solidarités à Paris au XVIIIe siècle* Paris 1986

– *Vivre dans la rue à Paris au XVIIIe siècle* Paris 1971

Farge, A., and M. Foucault *Le Désordre des familles, lettres de cachet à Paris au XVIIIe siècle* Paris 1982

Farge, A., and J. Revel *Logiques de la foule, l'affaire des enlève-ments d'enfants* Paris 1988

Faure, C. *La Démocratie sans les femmes, essai sur le libéralisme en France* Paris 1985

Ferret, Marc 'Les Tribunaux de famille dans le district de Montpellier (1790–an IV)' Thèse de droit, Montpellier 1936

Flandrin, J.G. *L'Eglise et le contrôle des naissances* Paris 1970

Fleury Michel, and Pierre Valmary 'Les Progrès de l'instruction élémentaire de Louis XIV à Napoleon III d'après l'enquête de Louis Maggiolo (1887–1879)' *Population* 12 (1957) 71–92

Foquet, C., *La Femme au temps de la Révolution* Paris 1989

Forrest, A. *The French Revolution and the Poor* Oxford 1981

Fortuné, F. 'Sexualité hors mariage à l'époque révolutionnaire: les mères des enfants de la nature' in *Droit et réalités sociales de la sexualité* Actes du Colloque de Toulouse 1987

Frank, L., *Essai sur la condition politique de la femme* Paris 1892

Furet, F., and M. Ozouf *Dictionnaire critique de la Révolution française* Paris 1988

Fuoc, Renée *La Réaction thermidorienne à Lyon (1795)* Lyon 1957

Gallerand, J. *Les Cultes sous la Terreur en Loire et Cher* Blois 1928

Garaud, Marcel *La Révolution française et la famille* Paris 1978

Garden, M. *Lyon et les Lyonnais au XVIIIe siècle* Paris 1974

Gelbart, N.R. *Feminine and Opposition Journalism in Old Regime France: Le Journal des dames* Berkeley 1988

Gendron, F. *La Jeunesse dorée* Quebec 1979

George, Margaret. 'The "World Historical Defeat" of the Républicaines Révolutionnaires' *Science and Society* 40/4 (Winter 1976–7) 410–37

Gerbaux, F. 'Les Femmes soldats pendant la Révolution' *La Révolution française* 47 (1904) 47–61

Gillett, M.C.R. *Hospital Reform in the French Revolution* UMI; Michigan 1980

Giraud, Léon *Essai sur la condition des femmes au point de vue de l'exercise des droits publics et politiques* Paris 1891

Girault, Charles *Le Clergé Sarthois face au serment constitutionnel* Laval 1959

Godechot, Jacques *Les Institutions de la France sous la Révolution et l'Empire* Paris 1969
– *Le Prise de la Bastille* Paris 1965
Godel, J. *La Reconstruction concordataire dans le diocèse de Grenoble après la Révolution (1802–1809)* Grenoble 1968
Godineau, D. 'Autour du mot citoyenne' *Mots* 16 (1988) 91–110
– *Citoyennes Tricoteuses: Les Femmes du peuple à Paris pendant la Révolution française* Aix 1988
– 'Formation d'un mythe contre-révolutionnaire: Les "Tricoteuses"' *l'Image de la Révolution* Actes du Congrès mondial III Oxford 1989
Goncourt, E. de, and J. de Goncourt *The Woman of the Eighteenth Century* trans Le Clercq and Roeder. New York 1927
Gonnet, E. *Essai sur l'histoire du diocèse du Puy en Velay (1789–1802)* Paris 1907
Gouesse, Jean-Marie 'Parenté, famille et mariage en Normandie aux XVIIe et XVIIIe siècles. Présentation d'une source et d'une enquête' *Annales: économie, sociétés, civilisations* 27/4–5 (July–Oct 1972) 1139–54
Gouges, Olympe de *Oeuvres* ed. B. Groule. Paris 1989
Graham, Ruth 'Loaves and Liberty: Women in the French Revolution' in *Becoming Visible* ed. R. Bridenthal and Koonz, 238–54. Boston 1977
– 'Rousseau's Sexism Revolutionized' in *Woman in the 18th Century and Other Essays* ed P. Fritz and R. Morton 127–39. Toronto 1976
Groult, F. *Une Congrégation salesienne: Les Soeurs de Saint Joseph du Puy en Velay* Le Puy 1930
Guibert-Sledziewski, E. 'La Femme, objet de la Revolution' *Annales historiques de la Révolution française* 267 (1987) 1–16
– 'Naissance de la femme civile' *Pensé* 238 (mars–avril 1989) 34–48
Guillaume, J. *Procès-verbaux du Comité d'Instruction Publique de la Convention Nationale* 6 vols. Paris 1898–1907
Gulickson, G. *Spinners and Weavers of Auffray* Cambridge 1986
Gutwirth, M. *Madame de Stael: Novelist* Urbana 1978
Hardy, S. *Mes loisirs, ou journal des événements tels qu'ils par-*

viennent à ma conaissance Bibliothèque Nationale de Paris, Fonds Français, No. 6680–6687; Paris 1789

Harris, Jennifer 'The Red Cap of Liberty: A Study of Dress Worn by French Revolutionary Partisans, 1789–1794' *Eighteenth-Century Studies* 14/3 (Spring 1981) 283–312

Hatzfeld, H. *Du Paupérisme à la Securité sociale: Essai sur les origines de la Sécurité sociale en France, 1850–1940* Paris 1971

Hufton, Olwen *Bayeux in the Late Eighteenth Century* Oxford 1967

– 'The French Church' in *Church and Society in Catholic Europe of the Eighteenth Century* ed W.J. Callahan and D. Higgs 13–33. Cambridge 1979

– *The Poor of Eighteenth Century France, 1750–1789* Oxford 1974

– 'The Reconstruction of a Church 1796–1801' in *Beyond the Terror* ed G. Lewis and C. Lucas 21–53. Cambridge 1981

– 'Women and the Family Economy in Eighteenth-Century France' *French Historical Studies* 9 (Spring 1975) 1–22

– 'Women in Revolution' *Past and Present* 53 (1971) 90–108

Hufton, Olwen, and Frank Tallet 'Communities of Women, the Religious Life, and Public Service in Eighteenth-Century France' in *Connecting Spheres* ed M. Boxer, J. Quataert. Oxford 1987

Hunt, Lynn 'Engraving the Republic: Prints and Propaganda in the French Revolution' *History Today* 30 (October 1980) 11–17

– ed *The New Cultural History* Berkeley 1989

Hunt, M., M. Jacob, P. Jack, M. and R. Perry, *Women and the Enlightenment* New York 1984

Imbert, J. *Le Droit hospitalier de la Révolution et de l'Empire* Paris 1954

Jaulerry, Eliane 'Les Dissolutions d'union en France étudiées à partir des minutes de jugement' *Population* XXVI (1971) 143–72

Jimack, P.D. 'The Paradox of Sophie and Julie: Contemporary Responses to Rousseau's Ideal Wife and Ideal Mother' in *Women and Society in Eighteenth Century France: Essays in Honour of John Stephenson Spink* ed E. Jacobs. London 1979

Join-Lambert, M. 'La Pratique religieuse dans le diocèse de Rouen de 1707–1789' *Annales de Normandie* V (1955), 35–48

Jones, Colin *The Charitable Imperative: Hospitals and Nursing in Ancien Régime and Revolutionary France* London 1989

– *Charity and 'Bienfaisance': The Treatment of the Poor in The Montpellier Region, 1740–1815* Cambridge 1982

Kaplan, Stephen *Bread, Politics and Political Economy in the Reign of Louis XV* 2 vols. The Hague 1976

– *Provisioning Paris* Ithaca, 1984

Kaplow, J. *Les Noms des rois, les pauvres de Paris à la veille de la Révolution* Paris 1974

Keohane, Nannerl O. '"But for Her Sex ..." The Domestication of Sophie' *University of Ottawa Quarterly* 49/3–4 (July–October 1979) 390–400

Kniebieler, Y., and C. Fouquet *La Femme et les médecins* Paris 1983

Lacour, Léopold *Les Origines du Féminisme contemporain, trois femmes de la Revolution: Olympe de Gouges, Théroigne de Méricourt, Rose Lacombe* Paris 1900

Lairtullier, A. *Les Femmes célèbres de 1789–1795* Paris 1900

Lallemand,L. *Histoire des enfants abandonés et délaisés* Paris 1885

– *La Révolution et les pauvres* Paris 1898

Lalou, Henri 'Le Remariage des divorcés' *Le Correspondant* (25 August 1930) 567–89

Landes, Joan B. *Women and the Public Sphere in the Age of the French Revolution* Ithaca 1989

Langeron, G. 'Le Club des femmes de Dijon pendant la Révolution' in *La Revolution en Côte d'Or* 5–71. Dijon 1929

Lapied, Martine 'Les Formes d'interventions populaires dans la révolution avignonaise et comtadine des émeutes du printemps 1789 aux massacres de la Glacière (octobre 1791)' *Actes du Colloque de Montpellier: Les Practiques politiques en Provence à l'époque de la Révolution* Publication de l'Université Paul Valéry de Montpellier 1985

– 'Les massacres révolutionnaires sont-ils des événements? Réflexion sur les massacres de la Glacière à Avignon' *Actes du Colloque 'L'Evènement'* Université de Provence 1986

– 'Les Mouvements populaires à Avignon et dans le Comtat Venaissin au XVIIIe siècle' *Provence historique* 145 (1986)

– 'La question religieuse et le refus de la France révolutionnaire dans le Comtat Venaissin' *Colloque de Nimes* 1989 'Religion, Révolution et contre-révolution dans le Midi' Paris 1981

– 'Les Sociétés populaires comtadines: Un test dans l'étude des option collective' *Annales historiques de la Révolution française* 266 (1986)

– 'Les victimes de la Commission Populaire d'Orange' *Colloque* 'La Révolution française et la Mort' Toulouse 1989

Langlois, C. *Le Catholicisme au féminin: Les Congrégations françaises à Supérieure Générale au XIXe siècle* Paris 1984

– 'Les Effectifs des congrégations féminines au XIXe siècle: de l'enquête statistique à l'histoire quantitative' *Revue historique de l'Eglise de France* 1974

Lasserre, A. *La Participation collective des femmes pendant la Révolution française; les antécédents du féminisme* Paris 1906

Lautard, J.B. *La Maison des fous de Marseille: Essai historique et statistique sur cet établissement depuis sa fondation en 1699 jusqu'en 1837* Marseille 1840

Le Brun, F. ed. *Histoire des Catholiques en France du XV siècle jusqu'à nos jours* Toulouse 1980

Le Moign Klipffel, A. *Les Filles de la Sagesse* Paris 1947

Leclerq, Dom *Les Journées d'octobre* Paris 1924

Ledré, C. *Le Culte caché sous la Révolution: Les Missions de l'Abbé Linsolas* Paris 1949

Lefebvre, G. 'Foules révolutionnaires' *Etudes sur la Révolution française* (1934) 1–26

– 'Pauvreté et assistance dans le district de Douai, 1788–an V *Positions des thèses de l'Ecole de Chartres* 1955

– *Les Paysans du Nord* Bari 1959

Lenôtre, G. *Le Mysticisme révolutionnaire, Robespierre et la Mère de Dieu* 2nd ed, ed P. Nora. Paris 1984

Léonard, Jacques *Les Médecins de L'Ouest au XIXe siècle* Paris–Lille 1977

Levy, Darlene Gay, Harriet Applewhite, and Mary Durham Johnson, eds and trans *Women in Revolutionary Paris, 1789–1795, Selected Documents* Urbana 1979

Lewis, G., and C. Lucas *Beyond the Terror* Cambridge 1983

Loraux, N. *Les Enfants d'Athéna, idées athéniennes sur la citoyenneté et la division des sexes* Paris 1981
– *Façons tragiques de tuer une femme* Paris 1985
– *Madame ou Mademoiselle? Itinéraires de la solitude des femmes, XVIII-XIX siècles* ed A. Farge and C. Klapisch. Paris 1984
Lovie, J. *Les Diocèses de Chambéry, Tarentaise, Maurienne* Paris 1979
Lucas, C. 'The Crowd in the French Revolution Revisited' *Journal of Modern History* 61 (1988) 421–57
– 'Resistances populaires à la Révolution dans le Sud-Est' in *Mouvements populaires et conscience sociale* ed J. Nicolas, 473–85. Paris 1985
Lyons, M. *France under the Directory* Cambridge 1975
Lytle, Scott H. 'The Second Sex (September 1793)' *Journal of Modern History* 26 (1955) 14–26
McCloy, Shelby T. 'Charity Workshops for Women, Paris, 1790–1795' *Social Service Review* 11 (1937) 275–84
McLaren, Angus 'Abortion in France' *French Historical Studies* 10 (Spring 1978) 461–85
Marand-Fouquet, Catherine *La Femme au temps de la Révolution* Paris 1989
Markov, Walter, and Albert Soboul *Die Sansculotten von Paris: Dokumente zur Geschichte der Volksbewegung, 1793–1794* Berlin and Paris 1957
Mason, Amelia Gere *The Women of the French Salons* New York 1891
Mathiez, A. *Le Club des Cordeliers pendant la crise de Varennes et le massacre du Champ de Mars* Paris 1910, reprint Geneva 1975
– *Contribution à l'histoire réligieuse de la Révolution française* Paris 1907
– 'Etude critique des journées 5/6 octobre' *Revue Historique* 67–9 (1898–9) 241–81
– 'Les femmes et la Revolution' *Annales Révolutionnaires* (1908) 303–5
– *La Question réligieuse sous la Révolution française* Paris 1929
– *La Vie chère et le mouvement social sous la Terreur* Paris 1927, reprint 1973

Mauzi, R. *L'Idée de bonheur au XVIII siècle dans la littérature et la pensée française* Paris 1960, reprint Paris and Geneva 1979

Mazauric, C. *Jacobinisme et Révolution* Paris 1984

Meyer, J.C. *La Vie religieuse en Haute-Garonne (1789–1801)* Association des Publications de l'Université de Toulouse – Le Mirail 1982

Michaud, S., *Muse et Madone, visage de la femme de la Révolution française aux apparitions de Lourdes* Paris 1984

Michelet, Jules *The Women of the French Revolution* trans Meta Robets Penington. Philadelphia 1855

Misermont, L. *Les Filles de la Charité d'Arras, 1794* Cambrai 1901

Molette, C. *Guide des sources de l'histoire des congrégations féminines françaises de vie active* Paris 1974

Monin, H. *L'Etat de Paris en 1789* Paris 1889

Monnier, R. *Le Faubourg Saint Antoine (1789–1815)* Paris 1981

– *Le Mort de Marat* sous la direction de J.C. Bonnet. Paris 1986 (esp. J. Guilhamou's article)

– *Mouvements populaires et conscience sociale, XVI–XIX siècles* Paris 1985

Okin, Susan Moller. *Women in Western Political Thought* Princeton 1979

Ozouf, M. *La Fête révolutionnaire* Paris 1976

Parturier, L. *L'Assistance à Paris sous l'ancien régime et pendant la Révolution* Paris 1897

Patrick, Alison *The Men of the First French Republic* Baltimore and London 1972

Perin, N. 'La Religion populaire: mythes et réalités. L'exemple du diocèse de Reims sous l'ancien régime' *Colloques Internationaux du Centre National de la Recherche Scientifique* 576 (Paris 1979) 221–8

Perrin, H. 'Le Club de Femmes de Besançon' *Annales Révolutionnaires* 1917: 629–53; 1918; 37–63, 505–32, 645–72

Perrot, M. 'La Femme populaire rebelle' *Histoire sans qualités* ed. C. Dufrancatel, A. Farge, and C. Faure. Paris 1979

– 'Les Images de la femme' *Le Debat* 3 (1980)

– 'Sur l'histoire des femmes en France' *Revue du Nord* LXVIII (1981)

Petersen, Susanne *Die Grosse Revolution und die kleine Leute* Köln 1989
- *Lebensmittelfrage und revolutionare Politik in Paris, 1792–1793* Munich 1979 ·
- *Marktweiber und Amazones: Frauen in der Französischen Revolution* Köln 1989

Petitfrère, C. *Bleus et Blancs d'Anjou (1789–1793)* 2 vols. Lille 1979
- *L'Oeil du maître: Maîtres et serviteurs de l'époque classique au romantisme* Brussels 1986

Phan, M.C. 'Les Déclarations de grossesse en France (XVI–XVIIIe siècles); essai instutionnel' *Revue d'histoire moderne et contemporaine* 1975: 61–88

Phillips, Roderick *Family Breakdown in Late Eighteenth-Century France* Oxford 1981

Pillorget, René, and Suzanne Pillorget 'Les Messes clandestines en France entre 1793 et 1802' *Université d'Angers centre de Recherches d'Histoire Religieuse et de l'histoire des Idées: Histoire de la Messe XVII–XIX siècle* Angers 1979

Plongeron, B. *Conscience religieuse en Révolution* Paris 1969
- 'Le Fait religieux dans l'histoire de la Révolution: objets, méthodes, voies nouvelles' *Voies nouvelles pour la Revolution Française* Colloque Albert Mathiez-Georges Lefebvre, 1974. Paris 1978
- *Pratiques de la lecture* ed R. Chartier. Paris–Marseille 1985

Pope, Barbara Corrada 'The Influence of Rousseau's Ideology of Domesticity' in *Connecting Spheres* ed M. Boxer and J. Quataert 136–45. Oxford 1987
- 'Revolution and Retreat: Upper-Class French Women after 1789' in *Women, War and Revolution* ed Carol R. Berkin and Clara M. Lovett, 215–36. New York and London 1980

Procédure Criminelle instructe au Châtelet de Paris sur la dénonciation des faits arrivés à Versailles dans la journée du 6 octobre 1789 Paris 1790

Quéniart, J. *Culture et société urbaine dans la France de l'Ouest au XVIIIe siècle* Paris 1978
- *Les Hommes, l'Eglise et Dieu dans la France du XVIIIe siécle* Paris 1978

Rambaud, P. L'Assistance publique à Poitiers jusqu'à l'an V Paris 1914

Rancière, J. La Nuit des prolétaires, Archives du rêve ouvrier Paris 1981

Reinhard, M. La Chute de la royauté Paris 1969
– Le Département de la Sarthe sous le régime directorial Le Mans 1936
– Nouvelle Histoire de Paris: La Révolution (1789–1790) Paris 1981
– Religion, Révolution et Contre-Révolution Paris 1960

Rive, A. 'Des "ministres laïques" au XIXe siècle' Revue d'Histoire de l'Eglise de France 1978: 27–38

Rochaix, M. Essais sur l'évolution des questions hospitalières de la fin de l'Ancien Régime à nos jours Dijon 1959

Roche, D. Le Peuple de Paris Paris 1981

Rosa, Annette Citoyennes: Les Femmes et la Révolution française Paris 1988

Rose, R.B. The Enragés; Socialists of the French Revolution Melbourne 1966
– 'Women and the French Revolution: The Political Activity of Parisian Women 1789–1794' University of Tasmania Occasional Papers 5 (1976)

Roudinesco, Elizabeth Théroigne de Méricourt: Une femme mélancolique sous la Révolution Paris 1989

Roux, M. de Histoire religieuse de la Révolution à Poitiers et dans le Vienne Lyon 1952

Rudé, G. The Crowd in the French Revolution Oxford 1959
– 'Les Débuts d'une idéologie révolutionnaire dans le petit peuple urbain en 1789. Esquisse d'une étude comparée' in Die Französische Revolution – Zufälliges oder notwendiges Ereignis? ed E. Schmitt and R. Reichhardt, 37–9. Munich and Vienna 1983
– 'Les Emeutes des 25, 26 février 1793 à Paris' Annales historiques de la Révolution française XXV (1953) 33–57
– 'La Population ouvrière de Paris de 1789 à 1791' Annales historiques de la Revolution française 187 (1967) 15–37

Rudé, G., and R. Cobb 'Le Dernier Mouvement populaire de la Révolution française: Les journées de germinal et prairial l'an

III' *Revue Historique* CCXIV (1955), 250–81

Sahuc, J. 'Notes historiques sur l'hospice de Saint-Pons' *Inventaire sommaire des archives hospitalières de Saint-Pons antérieures à 1790* Montpellier 1910

Schwartz, Joel *The Sexual Politics of Jean-Jacques Rousseau* Chicago 1984

Seligman, Edmond *La Justice en France pendant la Révolution* Paris 1901

Sévestre, Abbé E. *Les Problèmes religieux de la Révolution et de l'Empire en Normandie* Paris 1924

Sevin, E. *Les Missions religieuses en France sous la Restauration* Paris 1948

Silver, Catherine Bodard 'Salon, Foyer, Bureau: Women and the Professions in France' *American Journal of Sociology* 78/4 (1972–3) 836–51

Soboul, A. *Comprendre la Révolution: Problèmes politiques de la Révolution française* Paris 1981

– 'Un épisode des luttes populaires en septembre 1793: la guerre des cocardes' *Annales historiques de la Révolution francaise* (1961) 52–5

– 'Problèmes du travail en l'an II' *Annales historiques de la Révolution françaises* 28 (1956) 236–54

– *Les Sans-Culottes parisiens en l'an II: Mouvement populaire et gouvernement révolutionnaire, 2 juin 1793 – thermidor an II* Paris 1958

Soboul, A., and R. Monnier *Répertoire du personnel sectionnaire parisien en l'an II* Publications de la Sorbonne, Paris 1985

Sokolnikova, Galina Ospinova *Nine Women Drawn from the Epoch of the French Revolution* trans. H.C. Stevens. Freeport, NY 1932, reprint 1969

Soprani, Anne *La Révolution et les femmes* Paris 1989

Soucaille, A. 'Histoire de la Société Populaire de Béziers, d'après les procès verbaux de ses séances' *Bulletin de la Société Archélogique, scientifique et littéraire de Béziers* 15 (1890–2) 226–326

– 'Notice sur la maison du refuge ou du Bon Pasteur de Béziers' *Mémoires de la Société archéologique de Beziers* 1885

Staum, M. *Cabanis: Enlightenment and Medical Philosophy in the French Revolution* Princeton 1980

Stephens, Winifred *Women of the French Revolution* New York 1922

Stoddard, Julia 'The Causes of the Insurrection of the 5th and 6th of October' *University of Nebraska Studies* 4 (October 1904) 267–327

Suchet, J.M. 'Paysans franc-comtois' *Mémoires de l'Académie de Besançon* 1887

Sullerot, Evelyne *Histoire de la presse féminine en France, des origines à 1848* Paris 1966

Tackett, Timothy *Religion, Revolution and Regional Culture in Eighteenth-Century France: The Ecclesiastical Oath of 1791* Princeton 1986

– 'The West in France in 1789: The Religious Factor in the Origins of the Counter-Revolution,' *Journal of Modern History* 54 (1982) 715–45

– 'Women and Men in Counter-Revolution: The Sommières Riot 1791' *Journal of Modern History* 59/4 (December 1987) 680–704

Tallett, Frank 'Religion and Revolution, The Doubs: 1780–1797' PhD thesis Reading 1981

Tilly, Louise 'The Food Riot, as a Form of Political Conflict in France' *Journal of Interdisciplinary History* 2 (1971) 23–57

Tonnesson, K.D. *La Défaite des sans-culottes: Mouvement populaire et réaction bourgeoise en l'an III* Oslo 1959

Traer, James F. *Marriage and the Family in Eighteenth-Century France* Ithaca, NY 1980

Tuetey, Alexandre. *L'Assistance publique pendant la Révolution* 4 vols. Paris 1895–97

– *Répertoire général des sources manuscrites de l'histoire de Paris pendant la Révolution française* 11 vols. Paris 1890–1914

Turin, Y. *Femmes et religieuses au XIXe siècle: le féminisme en religion* Paris 1989

Viard, Paul 'Le Tribunal de famille dans le district de Dijon (1790–1792)' *Nouvelle revue historique de droit français et étranger* XLV, 242–77

Vidal-Nacquet, P. 'Esclavage et gynécratie dans la tradition, le mythe, l'utopie' *Le Chasseur noir* Paris 1981

Villiers, Baron Marc de *Histoire des Clubs des femmes et des Légions d'Amazones, 1793–1848–1871* Paris 1910
– *Reine Audu* Paris 1917
Vovelle, M. *Idéologies et mentalités* Paris 1976
– *La Mentalité révolutionnaire: Société et mentalités sous la Révolution française* Paris 1985
– *Les Métamorphoses de la fête en Provence 1750–1820* Paris 1976
– *Piété baroque et déchristianisation en Provence au XVIIIe siècle* Paris 1973
– *Réligion et Révolution: La Déchristianisation de l'an II* Paris 1976
– *La Révolution contre l'Eglise: De la Raison à l'Etre suprême* Paris 1989
– *La Révolution française: Images et récit, 1789–1799* 5 vols. Paris 1986
Warner, C.K., ed *From the Ancien Régime to the Popular Front: Essays in the History of France in Honor of S.B. Clough* New York 1969
de Watteville, A. *Législation charitable de 1790 à 1863* Paris 1863
Weiner, D.B. 'Le Droit de l'homme à la santé: une belle idée devant l'assemblée nationale constituante, 1790–1791' *Clio medica*, 1970
– 'The French Revolution, Napoleon and the Nursing Profession' *Bulletin of the History of Medicine* 1972
Wexler, V.G. 'Made for Man's delight: Rousseau as Antifeminist' *American Historical Review* 81 (1976) 266–91
Williams, David 'The Politics of Feminism in the French Enlightenment' *The Varied Patterns: Studies in the Eighteenth-Century* ed P. Hughes and D. Williams. Toronto 1971
Woloch, Isser *The French Veteran from the Revolution to the Restoration* Chapel Hill 1979
– *Jacobin Legacy: The Democratic Movement under the Directory* Princeton 1970
Woronoff, D. *La République bourgeoise de Thermidor à Brumaire 1794–1799* Paris 1972
Zeldin, T., 'The Conflict of Moralities, Confession, Sin and

Pleasure in the Nineteenth Century,' in *Conflicts in French Society: Anticlericalism, Education and Morals in the Nineteenth Century* ed T. Zeldin. London 1970

Index

Albitte, in Haute Loire, 116–17
Amar, and women's clubs, 37
Audu, Reine, 24

Barère, 33
Bastille, 7
béates, in Haute Loire, 116–17,
   137, 146

Chabry, Louise, 10
Champ de Mars, 20
charity, during the Revolution,
   53–8
Chaumette, 27, 37
Club des citoyennes républicaines révolutionnaires,
   25–39

cockade, affair of (1793),
   36
Comité de Bienfaisance, 84–5
Comité de Mendicité, 58–9,
   62–4, 66–70, 86
congregations: 61, Constituent
   Assembly, 3–4, 21; policy
   on church and poor, 54–70;
   71–7; abolition, 75–7; revival under the Directory,
   144–6
Convention: women's delegations to, 27; occupation of,
   28; riots of germinal and
   prairial, 42–5; laws against
   women's protests, 49; and
   the poor, 78–88

counter-revolution, and women, 95, 101–27
crowd, 6–50
cults, revolutionary, 118

Dames de la Halle, 36–7
dechristianization, 100–7, 118–19
Directory, problems, 134–6

égorgeurs, 130
enfants de la patrie, *see* foundlings
enfants trouvés, *see* foundlings
enragés, 25, 34, 37

feminism, nineteenth-century and the vote, 153
Filles de Sagesse, 74
Flanders Regiment, 12, 15
foundlings, 63, 82–3

germinal, riots, 43
Girondins, 24, 29, 30
Gouges, Olympe de, 23
grain issue, 13, 19, 21, 25–6, 28, 38, 40, 93

Hébert, *Père Duchêsne*, 21–2

industry, textile slump, 92–3

Jéhu, band of, 129

lace industry, 92
Lacombe, Claire, 31–2
Lafayette, 8, 20
Leclerc, 34–5

Leczinska, Marie, 15
Legislative Assembly, 21
Léon, Pauline, 23, 31, 32
Loi Chapelier, 19
Louis XVI, and the October Days, 10, 12

Maillard, 8–9, 16
Marat, 29; murder, 31
Marie Antoinette, 15
maximum, 28, 39, 92
messes blanches, 127
Méricourt, Théroigne de, 23, 29–30
Michelet, J., xiv–xxi, 138–40; and the Filles de Sagesse, 74

National Guard: in October Days, 8, 11; Champ de Mars, 20, 27; and riots of prairial, 44–5; and counter-revolutionary women, 117
nuns, and the Constituent Assembly, 55–9, 71–7

October Days, xix, 6–18

Paris: popular protests in, 5–50; Comités de Bienfaisance in, 84–5
Père Duchêsne, *see* Hébert
Pétion, and Reine Audu, 24
poor, 53, 62–70, 77–8
Portal, national agent in Haute Loire, 136–8
poverty, *see* poor
prairial, riots of, 44–7

religious observance: ancien régime, 102; Revolution, 103–11; revival in, 122–8, 135, 144–9; nineteenth century, 150–1

religious orders: and the Constituent, 54, *see also* béates, congregations, nuns, Sisters of Charity, Sisters of Saint Joseph du Puy, Filles de Sagesse, Ursulines, Visitandines

Republicans, and religion, 143, 149, 151–2

Reynaud, Solon, 114–15

rights of man, 3–4

riots: in Paris, 5–50; religious, in provinces, 124

Robespierre and Jacques Roux, 32–3

Roman Catholic church, *see* religious observance, religious orders

Rousseau, J.J., *Emile*, 4–5

Roux, Jacques, 27, 32–6

sans-culottes: stereotypes, 19, 21–2, 24, and cockade, 36; and maximum, 39; and the peasantry, 95–101

schools, state: failure, 136–8; in nineteenth century, 149

Sisters of Charity, 58–9; in Paris, 73–4, 81, 85

socialism, and women, 151–2

Terror, 25, 33, 40, 112–14

thermidoreans, 40; and religion, 121–2; problems, 134

Ursulines, 59–61

Varlet, 33–5

Visitandines, 59–61

war widows, 49, 78

wetnurses, 64–5, 82–3